Success
Without
Stress

LAWRENCE MITCHELL

Illustrator: Aryo Pamungkas

Cover Design: Chitra Bianca Appasamy

Editor: Heather Mitchell

For information about special discounts or bulk purchases, please visit www.rawenergy.info

First Edition
ISBN: 1514353563
ISBN-13: 978-1514353561

To Heather.
Thanks for always being there for me.

LAWRENCE MITCHELL

THE RAW ENERGY BUSY PEOPLE SERIES

Good health is our birthright; a universal goal that we all need to live our lives and achieve our dreams.

The Raw Energy Busy People Series is a range of hot-topic books designed to help you cut through the hype that is so prevalent in our modern times, giving you the context and practical guidance to enable you to become a healthier version of yourself.

CONTENTS

LAWRENCE MITCHELL

FOREWORD
by Dr. Annabel Boys

In 2001, I finally finished writing my PhD. I was exhausted, burned out, hated my subject and my body was sick. I had constant back and shoulder pain, regular 'stress headaches', terrible digestion and my husband and I were about to embark on fertility treatment as my hormones were all over the place.

My modus operandi was very simple: Focus on the goal, set a tight deadline and then work as hard as possible (get up at 6am, breakfast at the computer, work until I could barely focus, eat, sleep, repeat). This method had served me well for exams, teaching assessments, conference presentations and so on. There was the added bonus - so long as I worked as hard as I possibly could, no-one (least of all myself) could say I messed up.

But there was a spanner in the works of my winning system - it didn't / couldn't work long term. I was permanently on an energy rollercoaster, fuelled by coffee, chocolate and adrenaline. After each deadline I would crash exhausted and it would take a little bit longer to recover each time.

Burnout and stress are at the root of an extraordinary number of the health (and social) problems in today's world. If you recognise my story, or parts of it, as yours - you need to read this book!

Ironically, the PhD I was writing back in 2001 was on drug and alcohol use / abuse in young people and a large proportion of the 'subjects' in my studies were using drugs to help them to manage stress of one form or another.

The truth is – stress isn't always bad, bad, bad; in fact a little bit of stress is actually good for us as it can help us to focus and strengthen. It can even be a little addictive.

A few years later, post PhD and several major life events, a new job was the straw that broke my camel's back. I started suffering debilitating headaches (several a week) and was barely functioning. Now that I had a child to take care of, I knew I had to find a better way of working and resting that would enable me to do my best at work, without these peaks and troughs, while thriving in all areas of my life. I needed a system that was going to work for me long-term. After a lot of introspection, I qualified as a Body Stress Release practitioner (see Chapter 11), and then as a Holistic Health Coach.

It was through the Health Coach training with the Institute of Integrative Nutrition that I met Lawrence Mitchell. I remember being struck the first time we met by how jaw-droppingly productive he seemed to be! I was staggered by the sheer volume of 'stuff' he was getting done – seemingly effortlessly - despite holding down a challenging 'day job', having a young family and writing a regular blog and column in Men's Running magazine… yet he always seemed so energised and healthy and was nowhere close to burning out!

Lawrence is one of those people who totally 'walks his talk', and now I am delighted to say that he has packaged his 'talk' in this book. His style is engaging and easy to follow (even if you're not into the science-y stuff). So if you struggle with stress or work-life balance, making time to read this book cover to cover (and committing to putting the suggestions into practice) will quite possibly set you up for a very, very different future.

Read it now!

Annabel Boys, PhD
www.unlockmyback.com
www.healthcoachforwomen.co.uk

1 OUR STRESSFUL WORLD

'Burnout is the illness of the rich world.'
- Arianna Huffington

Welcome to the second in the Raw Energy Busy People Series, designed to give you essential practical advice to help you live your life well.

Living in the 21st Century is massively exciting on one hand, but highly challenging on the other.

It is exciting as the pace of change, driven by technological advancement, continues to accelerate, impacting every aspect of our day-to-day lives.

- We can shop and bank whenever we want.

- We work and collaborate with people all over the world in real-time.

- We can carry out research and gain deep insight efficiently, without ever leaving our desks.

- And we can reach and engage hundreds, thousands or even millions of people without spending vast sums on advertising.

Today, these are the things that we take for granted, and they will continue to evolve as we travel into the future.

But, as always, there's a price to pay.

What is exciting and amazing on the one hand, can be overwhelming and very stressful for people on an everyday basis, often leading to burnout and exhaustion.

So, as the pace grows ever faster, it's perhaps no surprise that stress is cited as the number one risk to our health, wellbeing and longevity.

Indeed, a group of centenarians were asked what they attributed to their long life. Whilst all of their lives were marked by stressful and tragic events, what they all had in common was an ability to manage their reactions and quickly bounce back to normality.

MY STORY

Having lived and worked through the Internet revolution, I have learnt so much - yet over the years have also struggled with stress and burnout in my quest for success.

My turning point came in the November of 2008.

At that time, I had just been promoted to Director for Marketing for RBI, a large information and publishing business based in the UK, and had taken on responsibility for over 100 staff, which was a huge leap for me in workload and accountability.

However, 2008 was not an ordinary year. It was a very scary time for many businesses and individuals, with stock markets plummeting around the world, and governments bailing out banks to prevent economic disaster.

For RBI, a traditional magazine publisher, things were particularly uncertain as advertisers started cutting their budgets dramatically and readers (and advertisers) flocked towards the web, where content was perceived to be free (and advertising much cheaper). With a burning platform and a big cost base, RBI had to make some tough decisions to get back to a position of stability and future growth.

On that ordinary Saturday afternoon in November, I'd just got back from a two-day round trip to Shanghai where my company had acquired a new business. On this cold, bright afternoon, I was out for my regular run, listening to music, reflecting on the week and making plans for the weeks ahead.

I stopped briefly to do up my shoelaces, when suddenly the world disappeared.

I awoke to find myself hooked up to a range of monitors, with doctors around me looking perplexed. In my shock and confusion, I remember thinking 'This cannot be happening to me!'

Having created and implemented a strict healthy diet and exercising regime, I had assumed I could do it all: I believed that I could work 17-hour days, travel globally, put my body under massive emotional and physical stress, and still emerge from it all unscathed! My body clearly thought differently!

After spending the whole weekend in the hospital, my diagnosis was an irregular heartbeat, caused by a virus I'd picked up in China. Once my heart rate had been brought back to normal, I was allowed to go home - though I was very lucky that there was no permanent damage to my heart.

I was once again free to live my life on my own terms, but this experience changed me - it forced me to stop and seriously consider my way of life and what was important to me.

I realised that healthy eating and exercise are important components of a resilient life, but are only part of the story.

I started to research what else was missing from my life, and as I learnt, I gradually made changes to boost my resilience. Over time, I have turned this knowledge into a suite of tools and techniques that I and my coaching clients use every day - and through the pages of this book, I now give that gift to you.

We are all different, and my goal with 'Success without Stress' is to help you find your own route to develop resilience, channelling your stress into productive energy and work that you can put out into the world to make the difference that only you can make.

Start where you are, and enjoy the journey.

OVERVIEW: HOW TO MAKE YOURSELF SUPER RESILIENT

'You are the lynchpin that holds your world together. Allow it to wear out and your whole world falls apart.'

Imagine a life without any stress at all.

Long, lazy days without any pressures or worries. No need to get up until 11am, if at all. You can do whatever you want, whenever you want. You have no responsibilities at all!

Whilst this picture may seem appealing to some, it doesn't take long to realise that stress isn't always a bad thing - and is in fact a very important part of life. We need an element of stress in our lives to rev our bodies into action and shape us into an appropriate state for the task at hand.

We need stress to get us out of bed in the morning and motivate us throughout the day.

'Only dead people don't experience stress'

However, whilst some is good, a lot isn't better! In today's world, people often feel like they have too many pressures and responsibilities.

5

Over a prolonged period, this constant stress will have a negative impact on their physical and emotional wellbeing.

According to Deepak Chopra, the health, wellness and spirituality guru:

'Stress is the number one epidemic of our time, directly or indirectly responsible for cardio problems and inflammation'

And Deepak isn't alone in this view. Business today runs 24/7 thanks to modern technology, but this 'always on' lifestyle takes its toll on the body, making it no surprise that stress is now a factor in:

- 75-90% of visits to doctors' surgeries across the globe

- 128 million lost working days in the UK alone, at a cost of £12.4 billion per year

- 40% of all medical insurance claims (tripled since 1991)

- 400% increase in adults taking antidepressants since 1988

Indeed, 40% of workers find their jobs to be "very" or "extremely" stressful, and 36% "often" or "very often" feel used up at the end of the day.

These stats support the view that stress is a big issue for us as individuals, business owners and governments. Moreover, the problem doesn't seem to be getting any better.

According to the World Health Organisation (WHO), if left untapped, stress-related disorders, which include heart disease and depression, will be the top two leading causes of disability in adults by 2020.

NAVIGATING YOUR WAY THROUGH THIS BOOK

This book is split into two parts.

In Part One, we will explore the topic of stress from a holistic perspective, examining what stress is, what causes it and how it affects our bodies, our families and our businesses - and what its impact could be if left unchecked for a prolonged period. You'll also get some historical context to frame your knowledge.

Then in Part Two, we'll dive into solutions, outlining how you can identify your stressors, cultivate the beneficial ones and eliminate or better manage the ones that are not serving you well. The key message throughout is that **you are in control** - you just need to choose to be!

Insights without action aren't much use, and so, scattered throughout the book are some useful exercises and tasks to help you put your learning into practice.

Let's get started with Stress 101, so we're all speaking the same language.

PART 1

STRESS 101

2 DEFINING STRESS

WHAT IS STRESS?

The word "stress" is so much a part of our thoughts and language these days, that it feels as if it has always been there. In fact, the term is borrowed from physics and was first used in its modern sense by physician Hans Selye in 1936. It refers to the body's non-specific response to an external demand.

Walter B Cannon had already shown that animals produce adrenalin in response to stressors - which was the first proof that the physical environment could trigger a bodily response.

Seyle took the concept one step further, identifying many other hormones that were produced in response to stress and demonstrating how these could have lasting physical consequences to the body.

So how do we define this ubiquitous term today? Flick through the Oxford English Dictionary and you'll come across a number of definitions.

'A real or imagined threat and your body's response to it.'

'A condition or feeling experienced when a person perceives that demands exceed the personal and social resources the individual is able to mobilise.'

'A failure to adapt to the world, and our immediate situation, as it is.'

'Nothing more than a socially acceptable form of mental illness.'

'A state of mental or emotional strain or tension resulting from adverse or demanding circumstances.'

For illustrative purposes, let's use the Stress Management Society's 'engineer's definition' of stress: *'Force over area equals pressure'.*

In other words, when a bridge is carrying too much weight, it will eventually collapse (and you will be able to notice the signs before it happens). The same applies to humans, with the excessive demands and challenges placed on us, and the 'collapse' will manifest in different ways.

It is worth noting that human beings cannot distinguish between real dangers and imagined ones. Both elicit the same physical response, which is probably why thrillers are so popular - people feel totally involved in the action.

Another word to highlight is the increasingly popular term **'resilience'**, which is the power to bounce back from whatever life throws at us. It acknowledges that whilst we will be given challenges and obstacles, heartbreak and grief, we have the ability to cope and carry on, and these coping skills can be learned... more of that later!

So.

Stress is the body's natural reaction to an increase in pressure or demands, stemming from a problem (real or imagined), turning into worry and anxiety and, left unchecked, potentially affecting our health and wellbeing.

It is also important to differentiate between 'stress' (the feeling we have when under pressure) and a 'stressor' (the stimulant or problem in our environment or mind that causes the stress in the first place).

The more stressors, the greater the stress!

So the solution could be to reduce the number of stressors in our lives - which, of course, is easier said than done. Or we could just alter the way we respond to them.

But we're getting ahead of ourselves, so before moving on, let's recap what we have learnt.

We now know that it's impossible to live our lives without stress, and even if we could, life would lack motivation, fun and purpose. We need, as Brendan Brazier (ex-professional Ironman, vegan creator of the Thrive Diet) labels it, **complementary stress** to regenerate our cells and achieve goals. This is the type of positive stress that boosts your energy and supports higher performance.

However, there's a tipping point, and too much stress isn't healthy. It's what Brazier calls '**uncomplementary stress**' - anxiety that produces no benefit and furthermore depletes our energy. This negative stress can come from the air we breathe, the food we eat and the thoughts we have, as well as the activities and responsibilities we find ourselves with. Throughout the rest of this book, when I refer to 'stress', I am referring to uncomplementary stress, rather than its more fruitful sibling.

So stress is a big deal. Let's now turn our attention to what we can do as individuals to protect ourselves, and as businesses to protect our employees. We should start by understanding the impact that negative stress has on our minds and bodies.

HOW STRESS AFFECTS OUR BODIES

Mother Nature, in her brilliance, has designed our bodies to be able to survive in the face of life-threatening situations (like all of our cousins in the animal world).

If a situation occurs, like a mugger snatching your bag, or you losing sight of your 7-year-old son in a super-busy tourist area in Paris (the latter happening to me at the Sacre Coeur last spring), your body's stress response, commonly known as 'Fight, Flight or Freeze', will kick in automatically to protect you and enable you to *fight* the threat, *run* (away) as fast as you can, or *stop* still and hope to be unnoticed. Total priority is given to the threat, to the exclusion of everything else - which has a huge impact on our heart rate, blood pressure and muscles, with all non-essential functions (like thinking) shutting down.

This response has been in place since the beginning of time, and though the stressors have changed from sabre-toothed tigers and woolly mammoths to problems relating to relationships, work, money, a major life event, a tough economy or fear of terrorism, the physical response is the same - and can heavily impact our physical and emotional wellbeing.

Contrast this with a restful state where your breath is deep, your body is calm, your muscles are relaxed; food can be digested more easily, your heart slows down and your blood circulates freely through your body's tissues, feeding them with nutrients and oxygen. It is not difficult to see how this state is most beneficial to the body's wellbeing.

Medical science has hugely progressed our understanding of the impact that stress has on our health. For instance, in the early 1980s, psychologist Janice Kiecolt-Glaser, PhD, and immunologist Ronald Glaser, PhD, of the Ohio State University College of Medicine, were inspired by animal studies that linked stress with infection.

From 1982-1992, studying medical students, they found that each year, during exam-week, the students' immunity reduced. They had a lower number of natural killer cells, which fight tumours and viral infection. Their production of immunity-boosting gamma interferon almost stopped and infection-fighting T-cells only had weak responses.

Furthermore, in a 2005 study of college students, Sarah Pressman, PhD, Sheldon Cohen, PhD, and fellow researchers at Carnegie Mellon University's Laboratory for the Study of Stress, Immunity and Disease, found that social isolation or feelings of loneliness both weakened the immunity of first-year students.

When you're faced with a stressor, your 'fight, flight or freeze' response is triggered by your reptilian brain (the amygdala), followed by the hypothalamus, which stimulates the adrenal glands to produce a surge of hormones such as cortisol, which can compromise the functioning of the immune system, and adrenaline and noradrenalin, which raise the blood pressure and make you sweat (see Hormones 101). Blood flow to the skin is reduced, making you go pale, your arms and legs are mobilised, and stomach activity is reduced (which can greatly impede digestion).

All this produces a physical reaction and sequence that you'll be very familiar with:

- Your lungs, throat and nostrils open up to allow your breathing to become more rapid, allowing more oxygen into your blood

- Your cardiovascular system leaps into action, increasing your heart rate so that more blood can carry oxygen to important muscles, allowing them to work harder for longer

- Your sweat glands open up to help you cool down

- Your senses sharpen to keep you alert to any threats, for example your pupils dilate, enabling you to see more clearly, and your hairs stand on end, making you more sensitive to your environment

- Your stored fat from fatty cells and glucose from your liver are converted into sugar for fast energy

- Your digestive system slows down to conserve energy, you may experience a dry mouth and maybe even loss of bladder and bowel control (in extreme cases)

- Your blood vessels contract to reduce blood loss in case of injury and your blood pressure rises

- Your immune system slows down (preventing and fighting disease is not a priority while under threat)

HORMONES 101

There are three important hormones that come into play during a stressful situation:

Adrenaline: 'The warrior hormone'. It's the first hormone to help your heart start pumping faster and harder, expand your airways, and secrete insulin to utilise glucose for energy - ready for action.

Noradrenalin: When your body needs to react quickly to a stressor, noradrenalin increases blood pressure, gets your muscles ready to escape or fight, increases alertness, dilates your pupils and causes you to sweat.

Cortisol: 'The spy hormone'. It kicks in within minutes to back up adrenaline and maintain high energy levels. It helps turn stored fat and protein into sugar for your body to use as fuel, and helps create a 'seize the day' heightened state and better memory.

IMPACT OF STRESS

Once the perceived threat has passed, your stress hormones and all bodily functions return to normal. However - and here's the thing - if you are constantly under stress, **these hormones remain in your body** and 'chronic stress' results. Your body stays on high alert, which affects your physical and emotional wellbeing in the following ways:

Skin
Stress can cause 'pro-inflammatory cytokines' (including stress hormones and other chemicals) to be released. This makes the skin more sensitive and more reactive, according to dermatologist and clinical psychologist Richard G. Fried (MD, PhD). This can lead to a range of skin problems, for example acne, blisters, psoriasis, breakouts, eczema and other types of dermatitis.

Head
When we are stressed, we often develop headaches or migraines. This is due to a build-up of tension around the head, neck and shoulder area. Stress can affect the brain as well. Research suggests that stress extended over long periods of time stimulates the growth of proteins that lead to memory loss and might cause Alzheimer's.

Individuals who are stressed also tend to smoke more, drink more alcohol and become engaged in harmful activities like drug-taking, all of which can damage the brain.

Stress is also in the same 'burnout continuum' as depression, and if left unchecked could lead to more serious mental health issues.

Heart
Because stress increases our blood pressure, there is a direct link with heart disease. Prolonged stress also affects blood-sugar levels,

which can have implications on the way the heart functions or lead to insulin resistance, which can result in type 2 diabetes.

The emotional effects of stress can also alter the heart rhythms or release inflammatory markers into the bloodstream, both of which could lead to a heart attack or stroke.

Stomach
Our stomachs are very sensitive to stress. Our brains and guts are directly connected via a system of tiny little nerves, stemming from the vagus nerve, which communicate messages between the brain and the stomach. Thus, the brain (and related stress) can easily affect gut function.

Stress doesn't only affect the functioning of the gut, but it can even change the composition of the microbes in the body (through a combination of stress hormones and poor dietary choices). Research is increasingly showing that **gut bacteria** help boost the immune system as well as aiding digestion. An imbalance can therefore lead to conditions such as IBS, as well as a compromised immune system.

Stress can also change the amount of gastric juices produced by the stomach. If you eat after a stressful situation, the nutrients in the food will not be absorbed as well as they would if you were calm.

Chronic stress exposure can lead to a variety of gut-related issues like gastro oesophageal reflux disease, peptic ulcer disease, IBD, IBS and even food allergies.

Intestines
Similar to the stomach, stress directly affects how well our intestines function. Stress-response in the intestines results in reduced nutrient absorption, decreased oxygenation of the gut, 4 times less blood flow to our digestive system, and a decreased

enzyme output by as much as 20,000-fold, all leading to less efficient digestion.

As you can see, stress is incredibly detrimental to the health of your digestive system and can even damage the delicate tissue, leading to inflammatory diseases and conditions like multiple sclerosis (MS), type 1 diabetes, rheumatoid arthritis, osteoarthritis, lupus, Crohn's disease, ulcerative colitis, chronic skin conditions, kidney problems, urinary conditions, allergic and atopic conditions, degenerative conditions, chronic fatigue syndrome, fibromyalgia, and a variety of other inflammatory bowel disease (IBS, IBD, etc.).

Interestingly, the connection between the stomach and gut actually works both ways. Not only does the brain affect the digestive tract, but the digestive tract affects our emotions. According to Harvard researchers, "A troubled intestine can send signals to the brain, just as a troubled brain can send signals to the gut. Therefore, a person's stomach or intestinal distress can be the cause or the product of anxiety, stress, or depression. That's because the brain and the gastrointestinal (GI) system are intimately connected – so intimately that they should be viewed as one system."

Pancreas
The pancreas responds to the 'fight, flight or freeze' signals by producing a more-than-required amount of insulin, which if consistently elevated (in the case of chronic stress) can damage our arteries, and put us at risk for diabetes and obesity - both of these can be forerunners of cancer.

Immune System
As we all know, the immune system helps to defend the body against foreign bodies like bacteria, viruses and cancerous cells. When we are stressed, chemicals that are released can suppress the effectiveness of the immune system by lowering the number of lymphocytes (disease- fighting white blood cells) available in the

blood, making us more susceptible to infections.

We all get stressed, and short-term suppression of the immune system isn't dangerous. However, when this stress becomes chronic and intense, the immune system is consistently compromised. The stress hormone cortisol, when raised long-term, renders the cells of the immune system unable to respond to hormonal control, requiring even more hormones to be released, subsequently leading to high levels of inflammation that promote disease.

Stress can also have an indirect effect on the immune system, because when people are stressed, they often reach for things to quickly reduce the stress - like alcohol, cigarettes, etc., which themselves negatively impact the immune system.

Joints and Muscles
Aches and pains in the bones, joints and muscles may also be stress-induced. Studies have shown correlations between increased depressive symptoms and reported stress with neck and shoulder pain as well as lower back pain.

Reproductive System
Stress is known to decrease fertility and sexual drive. Stress hormones like glucocorticoids lower the levels of a brain hormone called 'gonadotropin releasing hormone' or GnRH (the body's main sex hormone), and also boost levels of another hormone (GnIH) that suppresses GnRH – a double whammy for the reproductive system.

Women who are trying to conceive when stressed may have reduced success, as has been documented in numerous cases. When glucocorticoids are released in response to stress, our pituitary gland stops releasing follicle-stimulating hormones as well as gonadotropin luteinizing hormones, and thus suppresses testosterone and oestradiol production and dampens sexual behaviour.

SUMMARY: HOW STRESS IMPACTS OUR ORGANS

Head: Headaches or migraines. Long-term stress can lead to depression, Alzheimer's or dementia. Can also lead to poor habits such as smoking, drinking or drugs which can further damage the brain

Pancreas: Produces more insulin than required, which if constantly elevated can cause diabetes.

Heart: Blood pressure goes up, putting pressure on the heart. It can also affect blood sugar levels, which can impact the way the heart functions. The emotional affects of stress can alter the heart rhythm, causing an irregular heartbeat, leading to a heart attack or stroke.

Stomach: Brain and guts are directly connected. Changes in the composition of the microbes from chronic stress can lead to gut-related diseases such as peptic ulcer diseases, IBD, IBS.

Intestines: Decreased nutrient absorption, decreased oxygenation to the gut, less blood flow to the digestive organs, decreased digestion of food / other inflammatory diseases, such as Crohn's, colitis, chronic fatigue, IBS, etc.

Skin: Skin problems like acne and eczema

Immune system: Chronic stress will constantly compromise the immune system, leading to high levels of inflammation (the cause of many degenerative diseases).

Joints and muscles: Aches and pains in your bones, joints and muscles may also be stress-induced.

Reproductive system: Drop in sex drive, as well as drop in fertility, lower success if trying to conceive

Clearly, it is in our best interests to reduce and manage the stress in our lives as much as we can.

Stress will manifest in a range of ways for different people.

For instance, last year, I was dealing with a major restructure at work, my mother was having some serious health issues AND I was trying to complete a course. It was all too much and eventually, a serious migraine attack forced me to slow down.

Other people will suffer from stomach upsets, skin disorders or a weakened immune system in the short-term, or longer-term, heart disease, high blood pressure or another degenerative illness.

The important thing to note is that these symptoms are ***messages*** from the body, it's just that we don't always want to listen!

For your sake, please do listen.

3 CAUSES OF STRESS

A number of studies have tried to uncover what's driving our collective stress levels up. Some of these are macro, where we have little control, such as the global economy, the outbreak of infectious diseases, political uncertainty and terrorism, all of which are endlessly reported by the broadcast and social media networks.

Then there are the things that affect our own personal situation: relationships; health, work, money; and major life changes such as getting married, moving house, and changing jobs.

What's driving our stress levels up?

Money, Work and the Economy top the list, according to the American Psychological Association's 2012 'Stress in America' Survey, with relationships, family, family health and personal health following closely behind.

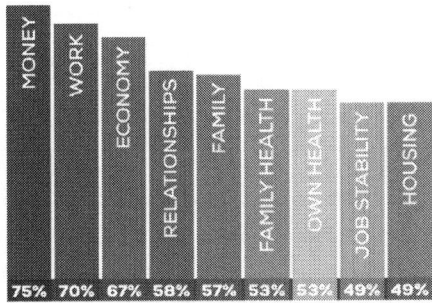

WORKPLACE STRESS

Whilst we all respond to stress in different ways, more and more studies are showing that corporate employees are amongst the most stressed of all.

For instance, a 2009 survey by The Stress Management Society revealed that 78% of the general working population claimed that stress was affecting their health, mood and sleep.

And according to Labour Force Survey, stress accounts for 40% of all reported ill health.

As well as affecting individuals in terms of their personal wellbeing, it's also costing businesses a significant amount: 128 million lost working days each year in the UK alone.

Whilst absence through sickness is one big cost, other less obvious costs include low morale & staff engagement, friction caused to others, increased staff turnover and work not being completed to a high standard, i.e. lower productivity and performance (or a term coined as 'presenteeism' - being at work but not as productive as you could be).

Led by the US, the good news is that companies are increasingly taking a more proactive stance to support their employees' wellbeing - gym discounts, healthy lunch options, meditation rooms, weight loss programmes, employee counselling services, running clubs, wellbeing fairs and other initiatives. These are specifically designed to educate, inform and support the whole employee community, not just those already engaged with their health, to help themselves.

And this investment is starting to deliver results. For example, according to Dame Carol Black, Department of Health's Expert Advisor on improving the welfare of working people: 'every £1 spent on workplace wellbeing can yield between £3 and £6 in gained productivity & efficiency'.

In a work context, the Health & Safety Executive has identified 6 areas that can cause work-related stress:

- The demands of your job – workloads, work environment

- The control over your work – how much say you have in the way your work is done

- The support you receive from managers and colleagues – encouragement, sponsorship and resources provided by the organisation, line management and colleagues

- Your relationships at work – includes dealing with conflict and unacceptable behavior

- Role – whether you understand your role within the organization

- Change and how it is managed – how changes (large or small) are managed and communicated within the organisation

Researchers have identified some common elements in situations that raise stress levels and have created a 'recipe for stress' interestingly shortened to NUTS:

- Novelty - new situations never experienced before

- Unpredictability - whether prepared for an event

- Threat to Ego - the likelihood of experiencing shame

- Sense of control – the ability to cope

The more *control* people have over their situation, the less stressed they feel.

4 WHERE ARE YOU NOW?

MASTERING STRESS

'Knowledge is power, and self-knowledge is especially powerful'
- Anonymous

As we are all different, and our lifestyles and personalities vary, it figures that we will not all be affected by the same stressors. In fact, one person's stressor will be another's motivator, and this changes and evolves over time.

Let me give you an example. Like many more introverted people, when I was younger, the very prospect of public speaking filled me with dread, and that fear held me back for many years until I decided that I had to overcome my fear and master the art of speaking in public if I wanted to progress and share my messages.

So I read widely on the topic, joined Toastmasters, trained with a speech coach, and practised like mad on groups of all sizes whenever I had the opportunity, until eventually I felt comfortable speaking to large audiences. Today, I regularly speak to groups of people and actually enjoy doing it, which at times truly amazes me!

Whilst I still sometimes do get a stress response, I now know how to channel it in a positive way.

In short, once we get used to a stressor, our comfort zones grow so we no longer get a stress response.

Technically this is known as **'habituation'.**

TAKE ACTION NOW!

Now it's your turn. Take a few minutes to list five things that used to stress you out, but no longer bothers you to the same extent. They could be situations like speaking in public, travelling in lifts, chairing meetings, meeting new people, flying, finding yourself face-to-face with a spider, etc. For each one, try to identify what caused you to no longer experience the same response.

Hopefully, this exercise has given you confidence in your ability to master stressful situations, as you've achieved positive change before, and can definitely do so again.

Let's now turn our attention to specific stressors that are currently in your life. Beware! This isn't as easy as it may sound, as the true sources of stress aren't always that obvious.

TAKE ACTION NOW

What are your current stressors?

Becoming aware of your stressors is the first step to removing them, so start by considering all of the things in your life that are causing you stress, worry and anxiety.

Don't judge, just write them down.

Now, for the next seven days, keep track of your stressful encounters and moments. A good way of doing this is by keeping a stress journal, noting down the situations, events and people who cause you to have a negative physical, mental or emotional response. Each time you feel stressed, note down:

1. A brief description of the situation: where you were, who you were with, what you were doing

2. How you felt both physically ('sinking feeling' or 'hot and cold', etc.) and emotionally (fear, anger, sadness, jealousy, etc.)

3. How you acted in response

4. What you did to make yourself feel better (if anything)

5. Then give the situation a stress rating of 0-10 where 10 is the most stressed you could ever feel.

The key thing you're looking to do here is to understand more clearly which areas of your life are the most stressful for you and the ways you tend to respond, both physically and emotionally. This way, you can take preventative action by developing a stress-reduction plan that is tailored for you.

At the end of the period, take some time to review and evaluate your notes by grouping your stressors into categories such as health, money, relationships and so on.

What patterns or common themes can you see? Are there any obvious causes of stress, or subtle or persistent causes such as an uncomfortable workspace, or a friend that drains you?

If you need help, work with a counsellor or coach who can listen without judging and help give you the strength to start taking action to remove the factors causing your stress.

TYPE A AND TYPE B PERSONALITIES

Friedman and Rosenman in 1974 identified two different personality types, Type A's and Type B's.

Type A's

- Competitive, achievement orientated. Self-critical. No joy in accomplishments.

- Time urgency. Impatient. Always on the go. Does several things at once.

- Anger/hostility. Easily aroused to anger, which may be overt or covert.

Type B's

- Low levels of competitiveness, time urgency and hostility

- Easy-going, philosophical.

Which personality type do you feel is most like you? Do you have an easy-going Type B response, or do you have the shorter fuse and more impatience of a Type A personality? Or are you a mixture, changing type in different situations?

Understanding the way you operate will help yourself and those around you know the best way to behave towards you to get the best response.

WAYS TO MEASURE AND TRACK YOUR STRESS LEVELS

If you're after a more scientific insight into how stressed you are, there are a number of ways to quantify and track your actual stress levels, which will allow you to see how often your body experiences a stress reaction throughout the day. You can then go back through the results and compare them with what you were doing when the measurement was taken.

This will lead to an understanding about what causes you to react with a stress response, so that you can take steps to reduce or remove those stressors.

TRACKING CORTISOL LEVELS

As outlined in the 'Hormones 101' section, a stress response causes your body to produce cortisol, among other things. So, by measuring your cortisol levels throughout the day, you can monitor exactly how stressed you are.

Cortisol is present in your saliva, so you just need to collect some on a swab, at different points in an average day. Specialists examine the samples, measuring the concentration of cortisol present. The results are charted (see figure below).

There are a number of places that can run the tests for you. I use Metametrix - Google for similar institutions in your area.

This is an example of the output you can get.

As you can see, my stress levels are somewhat higher during my workday, but they do come down on an evening....

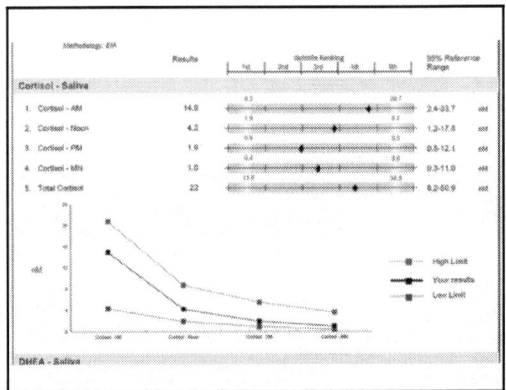

USING QUESTIONNAIRES

Other ways to understand what causes your stress could include completing a questionnaire or having a face-to-face interview with a trained professional.

We are currently running an internal measure of employee stress levels at work, which involves asking people to fill in a questionnaire that covers a diverse range of topics such as whether they are able to cope, whether they feel they have a healthy diet, how much alcohol they drink, whether they smoke and feelings about their work-life balance.

BIOCHEMICAL MEASURES AND PHYSIOLOGICAL TECHNIQUES

Another type of tracking device is a heart rate monitor such as Optima-life's First Beat Monitor. This tracks your heart rate and breathing patterns over a set period (normally a few days). It produces a set of charts of these measures over time, identifying when you are in a relaxed or stressed state.

I wore the First Beat Monitor on my chest for 7 days and only removed when I showered. During the week, I kept track of my activities and journalled how I felt. I'd selected a good week as I had some normal daily activities (like work), but also a couple of unusual events, including being a witness in court and running a 10k race. Busy week!

In my case (similar to the cortisol test), it showed that I experienced stress responses during the working day, but I managed to fully recover in the evenings and over the weekend. See one of my readings below.

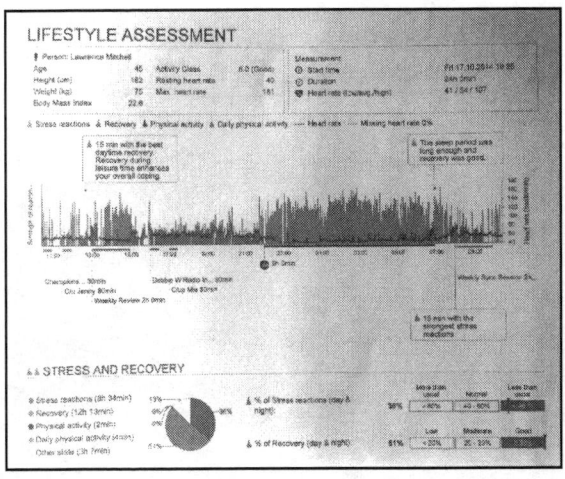

STRESS MOOD CARDS

Stress mood cards are portable, pocket- sized stress-testing products, designed to increase stress awareness. They use a bio feedback technology which gives a colour indication of a person's stress level measured by their body temperature: blue, relaxed; green, calm; red, nervous; black, tense.

SMART GARMENTS

Fashion houses, designers, "quantified self" enthusiasts and technologists are joining together to create 'smart garments' that provide tracking via tiny sensors built into clothes that come into contact with the skin, and so are able to measure and monitor a range of medical statistics and other metrics.

The smart garments can track things like your heart rate, breathing rate and skin temperature (which changes when stressed). Martin Ashby from Smartlife, which manufactures a range of smart T-shirts, highlights how these smarter garments are becoming increasingly used to aid performance in sports, and are gradually moving to support both personal and company wellbeing.

Like anything (especially at this early stage in their evolution) there are downsides. For instance, at the moment, some tools have standard 'average' settings - for example, in terms of users' relaxed breaths per minute - so some question the value of their insight.

Another and perhaps more worrying concern is what happens to all of this personal data, and I'd encourage everyone to watch 'Terms and Conditions Unknown' to get more perspective on this issue.

WAYS TO TELL IF SOMEONE ELSE IS STRESSED

Given the high presence of stress in our society, whilst having your own stress toolkit is important for your wellbeing, it's also good to be able to spot signs of stress in those around you. Here are 8 things to watch out for that could be a cry for help.

Stress can lead to people:

- Behaving out of character, such as becoming overly irritable or losing their sense of humour.

- Not sleeping, so looking constantly tired.

- Appearing out of control, unable to cope with situations they are confronted with.

- Feeling sick and nauseous.

- Being increasingly withdrawn, often isolating themselves.

- Having difficulty making even basic decisions.

- Being unable to concentrate on or finish a task before rushing on to another.

- Having irregular eating habits, including not eating enough or craving sugar and other unhealthy foods that lead to weight gain.

So, do keep an eye on your friends and family and support them if they seem to be suffering from stress. A friendly word or an offer of help can go a long way.

By now, you're aware that negative or uncomplementary stress isn't great for your long-term wellbeing. You've some understanding of how your body reacts to a stressful situation or thought.

It's now time to move to the next level and work through what you can do to protect yourself and boost your resilience.

PART 2

MASTERING STRESS

OK, now that we have some background on what stress is, the causes, and how to identify stress within yourself and on behalf of others, it is now time to look into ways of dealing with and mastering stress in order to live an optimal life.

When you walk through the second half of the book, digest the areas that resonate with you first and note down the ones you intend to take on board. Permanent change comes from a few small changes at a time, that are repeated daily until they become a part of your everyday life habits.

You, of course, need to *remember* to do them for them to become a habit, so keep reminding yourself to do them by setting daily reminders on your phone, using post-it notes, or whatever prompt works for you.

5 HEALTHY HABITS

MAKE WELLBEING A PRIORITY

The first step in any change program is to accept *responsibility* for your own life and situation. Wherever you are is down to all the decisions you yourself have made along the way. No one else. And, no one else can make your life better but you. Start by looking at how well you're looking after yourself from the inside out.

So many people are so busy with their day-to-day jobs and responsibilities that their personal wellbeing falls down the priority list. Remember that your true wellbeing is not the result of one thing, but the result of doing many little things which compound over time.

So let's break wellbeing down into its own toolkit, which will help build your resilience and enable you to take on more pressure without it going out of control.

HEALTHY HABITS, AT A GLANCE

Eat well

Drink well

Reduce unhealthy habits

Sleep well

Move your body

Do something creative

Laugh

EAT WELL

'Let food be thy medicine and medicine thy food.'
– Hippocrates

I am going to start with my particular passion - food and drink, not just because I am interested in food and nutrition, but because what we eat has a direct impact on how we look and feel. You are literally what you eat: the food that you take in, once broken down, becomes the raw material for each and every cell in your body. You therefore need the right ingredients to build a body that is designed to cope with our stressful lives.

Perhaps few of us would think about the nutritional stress we put our bodies under, by living off a diet consisting of too many refined foods, sugar and caffeine including junk food, white bread, processed meats, coffee and biscuits. You don't need me to tell you that these types of nutritionally barren foods are going to do very little to build resilience, and instead create their own set of problems such as increasing the risk of diabetes, heart disease and cancer. These diseases often stem from prolonged periods of an 'out of balance' diet, which our bodies attempt to compensate for, for a while, but ultimately, if not rectified, become sick.

Contrast this with a diet packed with nutrient-dense whole foods, either 100% plant-based or combined with the best quality animal products. No one diet will suit all of our individual needs, but logic tells us that a diet rich in whole foods, preferably organic and in season, will ensure good nutrition. I don't personally recommend removing any macro nutrient from your diet (i.e.: fats, protein, carbs), but I do suggest upgrading the *quality* of what you eat in order to maximise the medicinal qualities of the foods you eat.

So, a good, hard review of your cupboard and fridge is in order – anything that has ingredients your grandmother wouldn't recognise should have no place in your diet. It would also be worth seeking the advice of a nutritionist or naturopath, to ensure you are getting the right balance for your own body.

SPECIFIC NUTRITION TO SUPPORT YOU BETTER

There are a range of nutrients that you can take (via food and supplements), in order to help you manage stress better and boost your resilience.

Whilst my view has always been that you should be able to get everything you need from the food you eat, I have found that sometimes you need a boost in the form of supplements and tonic herbs from good quality brands such as Cytoplan or Lion Heart Herbs to provide that extra support.

Here's a list of some of these nutrients:

Joe Hibbeln of the National Institute of Health recommends eating **Omega-3s** to give you a more flexible stress system. Studies show that Omega-3s can help protect neurons against the damage that can be caused by chronic stress. Other studies show they alleviate depression as well as behavioural problems in children. You can get Omega-3s from oily fish (including canned sardines and tuna); also from flaxseed and chia seeds and from cold pressed hemp oils such as Good Oil.

Vitamin B-Complex works with brain chemistry and balances neurotransmitters. They provide a variety of health benefits including:

- Easing stress

- Alleviating anxiety and depression

- Improving memory

- Relieving PMS

- Reducing the risk of heart disease

You can get B-vitamins from dark-green leafy vegetables, animal protein, fish, milk, eggs, peas and beans, or taking a B-Complex supplement.

Magnesium is essential for dealing with stress. However, when you are stressed, your body gets rid of magnesium, so with continued stress, you gradually becomes depleted of this essential mineral. The lower your magnesium level, the more reactive to stress you become and the higher your level of adrenalin in stressful situations. Higher adrenalin causes greater loss of magnesium from cells (as well as all the other stress responses outlined in the first section of this book). So, making sure you have enough magnesium will improve your ability to deal with stress, breaking the cycle.

Foods that contain magnesium include raw chocolate, buckwheat, green beans, broccoli, spinach, oats, whole barley, millet, bananas, blackberries, dates, dried figs, almonds, Brazil nuts, cashews, hazelnuts, prawns and tuna.

Recent studies show that *Vitamin C* helps lower physical and mental stress. In Germany, 120 subjects were put under pressure in the form of public speaking and maths problems. Half were given 1,000mg of vitamin C; the other half were not. Those who did not get the Vitamin C supplement had higher levels of the stress hormone cortisol and higher blood pressure. Those who were given Vitamin C reported that they felt less stressed during the tasks.

Vitamin D deficiency has been associated, among other things, with depression, chronic fatigue, and muscle pain. Sources include liver, 15 minutes of sun exposure on the face and arms three times per week, and taking a Vitamin D3 supplement (also known as cholecalciferol, a natural form of vitamin D).

The amino acid *tryptophan* can boost serotonin (the "happiness hormone," important for regulating mood, appetite, sleep and cognitive function, alleviating depression and promoting relaxation). Animal products and nuts such as pecans, walnuts and almonds contain tryptophan.

Foods such as berries, apples, pecans, cherries and plums as well as garlic and onion offer the highest amounts of *antioxidants*, which are nutrients that bolster the immune system and protect the body against free radicals (nasties in your body, caused by stress, that can be the seeds for disease).

There are a number of *herbs* that contain compounds that have been shown to increase the body's tolerance of stress, such as rhodiola, ginseng, ashwaghanda and shisandra.

Ginger is also a powerful anti-stress hero, hailed by herbalists for its ability to alleviate headaches and inflammation. I make a delicious fresh ginger tea every morning. The recipe is on my blog **(http://bit.ly/gingrtea).** Other relaxing teas include chamomile and dandelion.

Finally, it's not just what you eat, but *how* you eat. Throughout my life, I've tried to cram as much as possible into my day - which often means that I just don't have time to eat and when I do, I wolf it down without tasting it. I'm sure you're not like me, but if you are, this isn't great practice.
SLOW DOWN!

Eating should be done mindfully, smelling your food and chewing each bite numerous times, savouring the taste. None of us are so busy that we can't stop for 15 minutes to eat and allow our senses to rise to the surface, enabling us to digest our food properly.

STOP WHAT YOU'RE DOING!

Don't forget to turn off the TV and your smartphone while you're eating, whilst thinking happy, calming thoughts for maximum digestive benefits.

DRINK WELL

Water is vital for all of your organs to thrive.

There's plenty of conflicting advice about how much to drink. At work, I see people valiantly making their way through what seems like three vases of water every day and spending the rest of the time running to and from the bathroom!

Whilst you definitely need to keep your body hydrated, you can take in a lot of water by eating a diet full of fresh fruits and vegetables, so do take your vegetable intake into account when calculating how much water you are drinking.

8 glasses of water / vegetable juice will be the optimal daily amount.

If you're eating a diet that is more clogging than cleansing (eg. junk food, refined carbs, etc.), try to get into the habit of sipping water throughout the day to keep your body hydrated. A good way of building more water into your diet is by writing down reminders to drink, or using an app such as 'Drink Water Reminder'

As with food, not all water is equal and you should strive to upgrade the quality of the water you drink, to build your resilience. You can find a good summary of the different types of water on The Raw Energy Blog (http://bit.ly/rawenergy-water), but as a rule of thumb, pure spring water and live vegetable water are at the top of the tree, whilst well water, i.e. 'common tap', is the lowest quality [just above 'puddle' <- joke!]

WHAT ABOUT TEA?

Tea usually contains caffeine so can dehydrate, rather than hydrate the body.

However, there's evidence to suggest that drinking black tea lowers the levels of cortisol after a stressful task compared to a control group (University College, London Study). The same research also showed that a substance in green tea leaves, L-Theanine, may shift brain activity from the beta waves that accompany anxiety to the alpha waves associated with relaxation.

TAKE ACTION NOW!

Track what you're eating and drinking every day for seven days. You can do this in a sophisticated way by using a food app like MyFitnessPal (although that is more about calorie tracking). Or you could just jot it down in a note pad! Note your levels of stress and overall mood alongside it, to see whether there is any correlation between foods eaten and feelings of stress.

REDUCE YOUR UNHEALTHY HABITS

Now it's time to think about the unhealthy habits you have developed over time to cope with stress, that may actually be doing you more harm than good. I'm not going to talk about smoking here, but do check Appendix 1 if you're looking for the support to give up.

Rather, I am referring to the things that we often feed ourselves to boost energy and cope, including refined sugar, refined flour, fast food, coffee or fizzy drinks, all of which produce a short-term energy rush.

Brendan Brazier talks about two types of energy; one from nourishment, the other from stimulation (like from the food items listed above). The energy from stimulation has to come from somewhere though. In fact it is only borrowed from the body, so the end result is fatigue, or **biological debt**. This puts the body under a lot of stress.

If you just did this once, the body would quickly recover. Over time, though, if this form of stimulation is continued, the body ecomes exhausted. To alleviate this, the body craves more of the stimulation, which is the beginning of a dependency (requiring more and more of the stimulant to have an effect).

This type of cycle causes insomnia, irritability, mental fog, lack of motivation, weight gain, lean muscle loss, premature ageing, and sickness. Over time, it can result in tissue degeneration, depression, chronic fatigue syndrome, and disease.

In addition, caffeine causes an increase in cortisol (stress hormone) levels.

Most Americans' (and other Westerers') bodies are chronically over-stimulated, without actually realising it. According to Brendan Brazier, 40% of the average American's stress can be directly linked to their diet. They crave starchy, refined foods, feeding the body more stimulants - and the cycle revolves again.

What your body really needs is for you to rest and eat a nourishing diet, without the stimulants, thus finally ending the cycle and allowing the body to repair itself and recalibrate.

If you're suffering specifically from sugar cravings and want to reduce the amount of sugar you're eating, download a free copy of my book 'Sugar: Sickly or Sweet?' (http://bit.ly/rawenergy-sugarbook) It contains a 14 step plan to get rid of any dependence on sugar.

TAKE ACTION NOW!

Start by tracking how much sugar and how many cups of coffee, tea and alcoholic drinks you're consuming, and then create a plan to reduce or eliminate them.

If you feel you can't do this alone, do get some help. There are many professionals out there who can help with different forms of addiction or dependency.

The important thing is to take action, so DO IT NOW!

SLEEP WELL

Whatever age you are, there's plenty of evidence to show that adequate sleep fuels your mind and body and helps you cope.

Whilst you're sleeping, your body recovers from the stresses of the day. Think of sleep as the mechanism by which your body restores its energy. So, when you get sufficient sleep, you feel more alive, your concentration is improved and you're able to function far better.

Feeling tired and lacking a good night's sleep contributes significantly to your stress, as it's harder to focus, your tolerance is often lower and you can feel generally irritable and off colour.

So how much is enough?

As with everything, we all have different requirements and the amount of sleep we need will change as we go through life. Generally, most adults need at least 7-8 hours of sleep per night. Yes, there are some people who claim to only need 3-5 hours, so if that's you, lucky you - you have four more hours in your day to be productive! Though, it is still worth experimenting and seeing how well you feel with more sleep.

But generally, 7-8 hours is the norm. Over the last year, I have been tracking my sleep patterns, both using sophisticated devices like the Jawbone Up, which tracks both quantity and quality of sleep, and also by just using a spreadsheet. I have discovered that I function best on 7 hours and 30 minutes; any less and my patience and response times are significantly diminished.

TAKE ACTION NOW!

Track your sleep patterns for the next 5 days and then try to get another 30 minutes extra sleep per day. Let us know how you get on over here: (http://bit.ly/rawenergyinfo).

MOVE YOUR BODY

'To deal with stress effectively, you need to feel robust and you need to feel strong mentally. Exercise does that.'
- **Professor Cooper**

Whilst what we put into our bodies is really important in building resilience, *moving* our bodies also plays a vital role in improving our ability to handle stress. I'll emphasise the word 'move' as oppose to 'exercise' here, as the 'e' word can conjure up images of gyms, joggers, and Lycra-clad cyclists - great for some, but can feel exclusive if you're not a sporty type of person.

Our bodies are designed to move, not just to keep fit and trim but also as a natural outlet for stress (and thus overall wellbeing).

Studies have shown that during exercise, your body frees itself of stress hormones and releases tranquilising chemicals (endorphins) in your brain, which contribute to your happiness. So whilst moving your body may not solve your problems for you, it will certainly help put you in the right frame of mind to do so. And often, important inspirations come to you in the middle of a workout too - so don't forget your notepad!

'But what shall I do – I hate gyms!'

Pick an exercise that you can make into a regular habit. Anything that engages the muscles or gets you up and active can work. For the past 15 years, my key activity has been running which, in terms of stress management, has helped me gain perspective on problems, leaving me with clearer thoughts and in a calmer mood (and often with a plan of action!)

If running isn't your thing, then there are a range of other options, ranging from swimming, cycling, playing football, lifting weights and doing aerobics, to even just a purposeful stroll in your lunch-break every day with a colleague or friend.

If you're pushed for time, try doing 20 squats, walking upstairs or squeezing a rubbery stress ball. And don't forget dancing – that often doesn't feel like you're exercising at all... until the next day! It is surprisingly straightforward to incorporate functional exercise into your everyday life.

Certain sports and pursuits such as skiing, rock climbing, golf or even table tennis, force you into the present moment – the intense concentration involved when trying to hit the ball, stay upright, choose the best technique, and so on, make you forget your worries while you're doing it – such a relief for tired minds.

DO SOMETHING CREATIVE EVERY DAY

We all have the potential to be creative, and even though some of us are more left-brained (analytic) than right (creative), throwing yourself into a creative activity is a great way to energise yourself and stave away stress.

Whether your 'thing' is writing, painting, cooking, playing a musical instrument, knitting or singing, make some time every day for these types of activities as they will help build your resilience and engage the creative side of your brain.

Don't feel particularly creative? Adapting your environment can make an instant difference. Having a walk and talk meeting at work, for instance, will make you feel different to sitting in a windowless office. Taking an hour or two to de-clutter your office can reduce feelings of being overwhelmed, as well as being very satisfying.

Similarly at home, surround yourself with soothing and uplifting photos and images such as beautiful scenes; or change the environment and hence your mood by listening to music or burning some incense.

LAUGH!

"To be intuitive, we must cultivate our sense of humour and look for reasons to laugh everywhere. We become so self-absorbed and serious when it comes to our problems and melodramas that we disconnect from our deeper sense of who we are as beautiful souls – we withdraw from life instead of enjoying it. Laughter brings us back to ourselves and back to life."
- Sonia Choquette

Some years ago, as an undergraduate student, I decided to do my final dissertation on the psychology of humour, and how humour and laughter can be used to achieve all kinds of wellbeing benefits.

Over the years since, more and more data has been published, supporting the compelling argument that we should encourage more laughter in our lives.

Laughter releases endorphins, which generate a sense of wellbeing and a positive mindset. It also decreases stress hormone levels and allows your body to automatically relax. Indeed, research suggests that a good, hearty laugh relieves muscle tension and psychological stress, leaving your muscles relaxed for up to 45 minutes after! It is also used in medical practice to help fight illnesses.

"You may not be able to change the situation that caused your stress, but you can change your reactions. Looking for the silver lining, seeing humour in your predicament, or regarding the situation as a test of your faith are all ways that you can manage your emotions and get through even the most stressful hassle."
- Susan Krauss Whitbourne, Ph.D.

I'm sure we've all been in many stressful and difficult meetings when a witty member of the team makes everyone laugh. Instantaneously, this has the amazing effect of changing the dynamic: defusing conflict, easing the tension in the room and repairing and promoting relationships.

So, with so many benefits, let's consider how you can incorporate more laughter in your life:

- Surround yourself with light and happy reminders. Frame your favourite joke, or a picture that makes you smile, and keep it in easy sight. I smile every time I see this picture of a gorilla who found a lost camera!

- Pay attention to children and imitate them. They are the experts on playing, taking life lightly, and laughing.

- Make time for fun, laughter-inducing activities. Watch a comedy, go to see a stand-up, share a funny story or joke, read funny books and simply do something silly just for the fun of it!

6 HEALTHY MINDSET

HEALTHY MINDSET, AT A GLANCE

See the positive side
Be your own cheerleader
What are you saying to yourself?
Play the Glad Game
Fill your mind with inspiration
Avoid the news
Accept what you can't change
Imagine the worst-case scenario
Set clear goals
Balance stressors
Failure is a chance to grow
Tackle fear head-on
Bad experiences balance out
Pre-determine your response
Have faith

GET INTO THE HABIT OF SEEING THE POSITIVE SIDE.

"Being miserable is a habit; being happy is a habit; and the choice is yours."
- **Tom Hopkins**

No situation is all bad. Stopping to count your blessings every day can make a massive difference to your mood and the way you view the things that happen in your life.

Take a leaf out of Alice Hertz's book. Alice died in 2014 aged 110 and, amongst other things, attributes optimism as being the most important factor of all: *'It depends on me whether life is good,'* she declared. *'Not on life. On me.'*

"Write it on your heart that every day is the best day in the year."
- **Ralph Waldo Emerson**

Life is like a pile of coins. Anything you come across always has two faces to it, and it will look different depending on which face you choose to look at. But the coin is still the same, whether you look at its bright or dark side.

'The average human being has 65,000 unique thoughts per day – 95% are the same as yesterday'
- **Antony Robbins**

'When you look for the bad in mankind, expecting to find it, you surely will.'
- **Abraham Lincoln**

'Seek and ye shall find.'
- **Matthew 7:7**

So, if you can focus on the good aspect of everything you do, task by task, day by day, you will experience considerably less stress and enjoy life a whole lot more.

One way to do this, as Eckhart Tolle reminds us in his bestselling book 'The Power of Now' is to keep focused on the present moment.

'The more you are focused on time – past and future - the more you miss the Now, the most precious thing there is.'
- Eckhart Tolle

Remember, a stress response is triggered just as easily by thinking of something frightening as it is by a real-life situation. So, by getting into the habit of thinking more positively, your stress levels will reduce accordingly.

'Change your thoughts and you change your life'.
– Dr. Wayne Dyer

Sounds simple, but changing your negative thoughts isn't easy, as often you're not even aware you're having them.

However, like any habit, it is possible to train yourself to be more positive about your situation, and below are some techniques that I have incorporated into my life, plus some resources and further reading for you to delve deeper.

BE YOUR OWN CHEERLEADER

'A significant milestone in life is achieved when you learn to be your own best friend'
- Jeffrey Benjamin

Is your ego your greatest friend, saying positive things when you wake up and all day long? That little voice inside your head, who is there to protect you, but who can also be your harshest critic, reminding you of all of the mistakes you have made in your life and holding you back from progress?

Many of us get into negative thought habits, where we tend to think badly about ourselves and our situation, berating ourselves for our mistakes, and playing the past over and over in our minds - which can literally bring us to our knees.

To change this mindset pattern, as with any change, the first step is to really pay attention to what you say to yourself.

WHAT ARE YOU SAYING TO YOURSELF?

"Why the double standard, the generosity toward our neighbour and the miserliness where we ourselves are concerned? And so I propose that we add a new rule, which we can call the Platinum Rule, to our moral code: 'Do not do unto yourself what you would not do unto others.'"
- Tal Ben-Shahar

Over the next week, really *listen* to the things that you are saying to yourself during an average day. It may help to write them down. Quite often, the voice is so subtle, so ingrained, we don't actually realise it is speaking!

Then to break the pattern, try to silence your inner voice by asking *'How is this thought serving me?'* A really simple question, which should help you stop the chatter for a moment, and allow you think in a more balanced way.

There's increasing evidence that those who look at their mistakes and failures with kindness and understanding, rather than harsh criticism, are happier, less anxious and more successful.

So remember that a dose of self-compassion when things are most difficult can reduce your stress levels and improve your performance by making it easier to learn from your mistakes.

PLAY THE GLAD GAME

Clearly if you're running out of a burning building, that isn't the best time to count your blessings, but in many of life's stressful situations, the Glad Game can give you a different perspective.

Whilst this may sound a bit 'Pollyanna-ish', it actually does work wonders and I play it every day before going to bed, and we enjoy it as a family at the end of the week, over dinner.

The rules are quite simple. List the things that you appreciate about your day, your week and your life right now. (At dinner, we take turns to name something we're glad about this week, until we can't think of anything else), There are no right or wrong answers.

It really is a powerful game, giving you the opportunity to see your life in a new, more positive perspective, and even allowing you to find good aspects about the areas that are not going as well. If you can't think of anything, don't forget to be glad about your family, your home, your health, your freedom - basic things that many people on this planet do not have.

Studies have shown that this simple act of positive thinking reduces stress. For instance, one study at the University of California found that those people who take time to reflect on the things that are most important to them, rather than on the things that mattered least to them, had a lower stress response. According to the study's lead author, David Creswell, PhD, by thinking about the important things in life, a stressful event became less of a threat and more of a challenge.

'The more you express gratitude for what you have, the more likely you will have even more to express gratitude for.'
– Zig Ziglar

'There is something about everything that you can be glad about, if you keep hunting long enough to find it.'
- Eleanor H Porter (Author of 'Pollyanna')

FILL YOUR MIND WITH PERSONAL DEVELOPMENT THOUGHTS THAT INSPIRE YOU

'You are a sum of the books you read and the people you come in contact with.'
- Jim Rohn

'All leaders must be readers'
- Harry S. Truman

There are so many amazing books out there, filled with a myriad ways of improving yourself and your situation. Take advantage of the great minds that took the trouble to put their ideas down on paper, and allow yourself to grow in the process.

There has never been a better time to improve your mind – and the Internet makes the information even more readily available.

I aim to read 4 books per month. Audiobooks make this task easier, making time in the car or train productive.

I also highly recommend watching the many **TED talks** **(www.TED.com)** that are available free online. They are short thought pieces given by the most incredible people on the planet, that never fail to inspire.

AVOID THE NEWS

If you fill your mind with negative news, it figures that this is not going to help lift your spirits. I'm not suggesting that you stick your head in the sand, however the news that is reported generally focuses on the bad things that have happened, rather than the millions of positive, wonderful, happy occurrences – news agencies know that bad news sells newspapers and gains visits to websites.

So if you do watch, listen to, or read the daily news, balance it out with a daily dose of inspirational learning.

For example, when I'm in my car, instead of listening to the repetitive news like I used to, I have turned my car into a 'Temple of Learning' and listen to Audio Books on personal development, business development and wellbeing which open my mind and challenge my thoughts and perspectives.

This not only means that when I arrive at my destination I'm in a far better mindset and mood, but it has also exposed me to many great books that I otherwise would not have had the opportunity to read; and most importantly, I arrive armed with knowledge and inspiration to move forward (and put the negative news into perspective).

If you're interested in personal development as a topic, you'll find a range of some of my favourite personal development books on the **Raw Energy** website (http://bit.ly/rawenergy-store).

ACCEPT THE THINGS YOU CAN'T CHANGE

"Through practise, I've come to see that the deepest source of my misery is not wanting things to be the way they are. Not wanting myself to be the way I am. Not wanting the world to be the way it is. Not wanting others to be the way they are. Whenever I'm suffering, I find this war with reality to be at the heart of the problem."
- Stephen Cope

Learning to accept what is, is an important coping mechanism. There are some things that you can't do anything about and trying to fight against them will achieve nothing and waste your energy reserves.

For example, during the dotcom boom in the late 1990s, I worked for a VC-backed start-up business. It was a wonderful experience, working for a very young company with exciting plans and lots of money to invest. The only problem was that it didn't have any customers, and wasn't recruiting new ones fast enough!

As was the case with many 'dotcom startups', before long, the VC backers decided that enough was enough and pulled their investment, leaving us high and dry. I was young at the time and learnt some valuable life lessons from the experience; but had to emotionally 'move on' pretty quickly as I needed another job and there was nothing I could do to change the situation. A couple of my ex-colleagues found it difficult to deal with and spent years lamenting,.

What are you holding onto that you need to let go of?

I know reading these words is a lot easier than taking the action, but learning to *let go* of anger and resentment, and forgive and move on, will release an enormous amount of built-up stress inside you. After all, what good will come of carrying the past around with you?

Try this. The next time someone does something to offend you - perhaps they sent you a direct and rude email, took your parking space, behaved disrespectfully in some way, or treated you very badly indeed - try saying out loud (not necessarily 'to' them), **'I forgive you'** (and truly mean it!).

Sounds odd, I know, but you'll benefit by deflating the anger and boosting your compassion. (After all, the only person that suffers from your feelings of resentment, is you).

As Nelson Mandela said:

'Resentment is like drinking poison and hoping it will kill your enemy'

Whatever has happened in the past, and whatever should have happened, is now over. Unless you are Doctor Who or another Time Lord, the past cannot be changed, so you simply have to accept what is - as difficult as this may be.

By doing so, you are setting yourself free from your past, allowing yourself to accept what has happened and then move on.

IMAGINE THE WORST-CASE SCENARIO

"Fear is an illusion. There are multiple different styles of illusion in the Fears cupboard, but at the end of the day they are ALL just illusions... They are all not real, so the only thing to conquer is the nutter inside your mind who is creating these things for you to be afraid of and then prodding and poking you until you become afraid."
- Andy Shaw

Many of us, myself included, have a tendency to worry. In the past, I'd worry a lot about the future and often reflect on past decisions with a good dose of regret.

Then one day, I realised that all of this worry wasn't helping me at all, so I took out my notepad and I listed the things that I was worried about and then wrote out the worst thing that could happen. This was a painful task as it forced me to face my deepest fears, but by doing so, it enabled me to work out the likelihood of that fear becoming a reality.

I then organised the list into what I could control and what I couldn't and was surprised that I could control a lot more than I thought.

Whilst, yes, the economy may collapse tomorrow (which is outside of my control), I make sure that I have sufficient supplies of water and food if the supermarket shelves run dry, and I am learning to be more self-sufficient by planting more healthy, organic fruit and veg.

On a daily basis, I reduce the risk of getting ill by actively applying nutrition and exercise in my life, and reduce the worry of my family getting ill by helping them focus on their own diet and health plans. So look at a worry for what it is – a projection of something that may not happen – and a guide to action on a certain area. Do something practical about the things that you can control or influence, and leave the rest behind. It is certainly not necessary to address them on a daily (or hourly) basis.

TAKE ACTION NOW!

Think about something you're worried about and imagine the worst-case scenario. Then consider the likelihood of it happening and start to brainstorm solutions.

Worry is born of helplessness and not taking action.

If you're worried about a current issue like your finances, take time to focus on the problem and work out a solution. A financial coach can work wonders.

SET CLEAR GOALS

Sometimes we can be stressed, simply because we're not clear on the outcome of our actions. This cloudy approach goes against the core human need for certainty. I see this often: people putting themselves under a lot of stress to complete a task without fully appreciating the reasons why they're doing it. Often they become so focused on delivery, that they take way too much time to do something that in reality wasn't that important.

To prevent this, I'm a firm believer in setting clear goals on what you want your life (or your project) to look like. The clearer you are on the outcome (and the feelings they will produce when you get there), the more motivated and engaged you'll be with the process. And you'll set yourself the right amount of time to do each task.

Similarly, when a goal is achieved, it's helpful to reflect on what you have accomplished, and celebrate your achievement. Psychologically, it's often not whether you've reached your final goal that determines how you feel, but the rate at which you are closing the gap between where you are now and where you want to be. It can be enormously helpful to take a moment and reflect on what you've accomplished so far, before turning your attention to the challenges that remain ahead.

Celebrate your success!

"Sometimes you need to step back and look at the bigger picture in life and you might be surprised at what you can see"
- **thatonerule:#1875**

BALANCE THE STRESSOR

An interesting technique from www.humanstress.ca, is to counter the effects of a stressful event by focusing on an equally engaging calming thought. So, if the boss calls you to come immediately into his office and you feel your stress hormones kicking in, conjure up a thought such as the look on your child's face when they were first able to blow out their birthday candles. This imagery modifies the gravity of the situation and should help to calm you down.

An NLP technique called 'reframing' could also be useful here. It is where you look for new meanings of a situation, for example, your boss may be giving you negative feedback, but it is in fact an opportunity for you to grow.

Another way of reframing a situation is to realise that one day we will all be dead... though harsh, putting things into this kind of context means things can't be all bad. [And this also teaches us not to forget to live].

WELCOME FAILURES AS A CHANCE TO GROW

Whilst most of us avoid it at all cost, failure, though painful at the time, can actually be a very good teacher. To fail and learn from your experience teaches you more than if you did everything right the first time.

"Failure is frustrating. But it's also temporary and eventually yields wisdom. We can think of failure as part of life's apprenticeship. If we were perfect and had all the answers, we'd never get to ask questions, and we wouldn't be able to discover anything new."
- **Kristen Neff**

There are many, many stories that bring this point to life. Examples where, had the leaders not had grit and the strength to carry on despite their failures, the world would never have benefited from their creations.

James Dyson, for instance, made 2,000 prototypes of his vacuum cleaner before he perfected his dual cyclone technology – you could say he failed 1,999 times. But his tenacity eventually paid off.

Similarly, had the developers of Angry Birds given up after their 50th attempt, they would never have struck success with their 51st version!

And 12 publishers rejected the original Harry Potter manuscript, until Bloomsbury agreed to publish it!

The important thing is to pick yourself up, take the learning on board, and keep moving forward on the path - staying open to pivoting if you need to.

TACKLE FEAR HEAD-ON

"No one is born with confidence. Those people around you who radiate confidence, who have conquered worry, who are at ease everywhere and all the time, acquired their confidence, every bit of it." - David Schwartz

What are you afraid of? What is it that you are putting off doing? Be honest, are you not doing it because you are scared of doing it? If so, consider this:

"Action cures fear. Indecision, postponement, on the other hand, fertilise fear... Jot that down in your success rule book right now. Action cures fear."
- David Schwartz

So, what is making you fearful right now? Doing your tax return? Writing a business plan? Writing your Will? Whatever it is, JUST START! The task is rarely as bad as you are building it up to be, and imagine how happy you'll feel when you've completed the task!

Brian Tracey in his book 'Eat that Frog' recommends us to do the Frogs (that is, the most important things) first, then work backwards. That way, you will move forwards rapidly, and your fear will miraculously melt away!

"Where does confidence come from? Great athletes say that confidence is knowing they are prepared physically and mentally. Experience tells them what to do and confidence allows them to do it. Confidence is the emotional knowing that you are prepared, mind, body and spirit, for anything."
- Gary Mack

BAD EXPERIENCES ARE BALANCED OUT BY GOOD ONES

Life is a set of experiences. Some may be considered as 'good'; others bad. The bad allows us to understand and appreciate the good. Taken as a whole, the good tends to balance out the bad. The yin and the yang – one complements the other.

We've all, I'm sure, had bad things happen to us which felt terrible at the time, but then resulted in something good coming out of it, either through a new learning, a new relationship developing, or another positive outcome.

When my wife Heather's mother died suddenly from a brain haemorrhage on Christmas Day in 2003, it was a tragic and awful period for us. However, that sad event brought her long-lost cousin Victoria and her family back into our lives, which led to many positive ripples in all our lives.

To be clear, this doesn't mean you shouldn't work diligently towards preventing what you don't want to happen. It just means that if the worst does happen, then you will accept it, deal with your situation and move on.

PRE-DETERMINE YOUR RESPONSE TO EVENTS

Changing your emotions isn't easy, but it is possible with the right healthy habits.

Like the centenarians who attributed their long lives to how they managed their response to stress, recent studies show that 'if-then' plans can help us to control our emotional responses to situations in which we feel fear, sadness, fatigue, self-doubt or even disgust.

Simply decide what kind of response you would like to have instead of stress, and make a plan that links your desired response to the situations that tend to raise your blood pressure. For instance, 'If I see lots of emails in my inbox, then I will stay calm and relaxed.' Or 'If my partner leaves the kitchen in a mess, I will take a deep breath and calmly explain that I would like things put away next time.'

Dr. Steve Peters, in his book 'The Chimp Paradox", says that our brain is divided into the Human, the Computer and also the Chimp. The Chimp is driven by *feelings and emotions* and so will jump to conclusions quickly and may have violent reactions due to catastrophic thinking. You therefore need to learn to manage the Chimp, in order to have a more evenly balanced life.

HAVE FAITH

This may sound a bit "woo woo", but I have edged closer and closer to my spiritual self over the last decade, not necessarily from a traditional religious approach, but from a more holistic spiritual appreciation.

Spiritual faith gives you a sense of peace, knowing that whatever happens to you will work out for the best, even if it may not seem likely at the time.

Alcoholics Anonymous uses faith as a way of curing alcoholism:

"Every person has some belief, more or less vague, in a creative, life-giving force, a universal mind or soul. Alcoholics Anonymous begins by thinking of this as a Power rather than a Person. It works unseen as electricity, may be thought of as gravitation, evolution, or growth. Thought is a power, good will is a power, and trust is a power. Trying to visualise the Higher Power is a hindrance rather than a help. Formulas are of little value. Like the wind, the spirit can be felt but not seen. Instead of expecting ecstasies, visions, trances, one finds God in what is; contact may be made through gratitude.

Surrender to the Higher Power is not difficult for alcoholics, because for years they have surrendered to a lower power."

From Religion in Life, Vol. 18(1): 25-33, 1948

Further Reading

If you're ready to tackle your mindset, three great books to recommend are Louise Hay's 'You Can Change Your Life', Andy Shaw's 'Bug-Free Mind' and 'The Chimp Paradox' by Dr. Steve Peters.

TAKE ACTION NOW!

Imagine a particularly pushed day. It takes 30 minutes to get to your next appointment and you have given yourself exactly 30 minutes to get there. When you turn onto the dual carriageway, you're faced with an enormously long line of stationary traffic. It is too late to turn back. You're going nowhere.

How do you feel? Note down your emotions. Chances are you'll feel frustrated, anxious, annoyed and other similar things.

Andy Shaw, in his book A Bug-Free Mind, encourages us to think of these 'forced waiting' situations as opportunities to reflect. For example, just the other day, I caught myself getting overly stressed as I was stuck in this type of traffic jam on my way to a meeting. I could feel my stress response rising as I anxiously looked at the clock and made mental calculations of the time I was likely to arrive. I stretched my neck out to try to see what was causing the delay, but couldn't see anything, just a line of cars, snaking into the distance.

Then I stopped, accepted the situation and chose to use it as an opportunity to play the glad game. This made a huge difference to me. My breathing slowed down, my shoulders dropped; I felt noticeably better. I then realised that I had some extra time in my Temple of Learning! Sometimes it's better to go along with Fate, rather than try to rage against it.

Try out this technique if you're in a queue at the airport or the supermarket, or any other forced waiting scenario.

'Instead of letting the frequent wailing of sirens irritate us, we could use the sound to remind us to take a pause and notice the moment. At the traffic crossing, instead of being impatient for the green man, appreciate how the red man gives us a chance to stop, breathe and look around.'
- Tessa Watt

7 PRODUCTIVITY HABITS

TIME

"Everything changed the day she figured out there was exactly enough time for the important things in her life."
- **Brian Andreas**

Without question, ***time*** is our most valuable asset and the law of time is something that governs all of our lives.

Whilst we all have the same amount of hours in our days, the feeling that we don't have enough time for everything we would like to do is a big cause of anxiety for many people – indeed, this is one of the biggest stressors that comes up with my coaching clients.

This feeling of being overwhelmed and drowning in lists of unfinished tasks can lead to the inability to cope and, unchecked, can spiral into depression. In this situation, it's very hard to stay calm and focused.

This 'Time Famine' as Adrianna Huffington calls it, applies to individual days and also multiplies up to our whole lives - so it is worth finding a solution, once and for all.

It is interesting to note that whilst some people whip through their lists, getting dozens of things accomplished, others find it tough to move off first base.

The good news is that with a degree of discipline and a few new healthy habits, this feeling of overwhelm can be replaced with a sense of control over your own life. True success in this area comes from a combination of 'mindset' and systems, both of which can be learned and mastered.

Good time management means quality work, rather than quantity, operating smarter by concentrating on the tasks that will make a real difference to your work and life.

Over time, and after studying what many successful people have done in this area, I have developed my own system for managing my time, which is underpinned by a process of planning ahead and creating good habits and procedures.

Consistently following my system has made an immeasurable difference to my stress levels and sense of wellbeing and productivity. Similarly my clients, friends and family who follow it have also found a new sense of lightness in their lives (not to mention, extra time to spend on leisure and creative pursuits).

HERE'S MY SYSTEM:

- **Accept** that you'll never get to the end of your to-do list. Yes, it will keep growing, but there's enough time for all of the important things and you don't have to do everything!

- **Simplify** your list by reducing the number of commitments to just the essential ones. Analyse your priorities and daily tasks and **distinguish between the 'shoulds' and the 'musts'**. Schedule only a few important things each day, and build space between them. Your goal here is to take things off and give yourself time back.

- Learn to **say 'No!'** – and slowly get out of commitments that aren't beneficial to you. Over the years, I have known many stressed and overworked people who continue to add to their loads simply because they don't know how to say 'no'. I used to be one of them!

I have also known a number of people who are very protective of their time and place firm **boundaries** between work and other aspects of their lives; not allowing others to 'steal' their time. This leads to more balanced lifestyles.

- Make sure to **allocate time** to read emails or watch 'time-sensitive' podcasts designed to pull you away from your agenda and onto theirs. It's very easy to get sucked in!

Andy Shaw in his book, 'A Bug-Free Mind', talks about having a 'Must **not** do list' as well as a 'to do' list, to help you focus on the 20% of tasks that add the most value to your life, rather than the 80% that don't. When you let go of something, you create space for something wonderful and unexpected to take its place. Identify key priorities by being ruthlessly results-oriented. Perhaps it's one of the great unfairnesses in life, but the first prize never goes to the person who works the hardest, does it?

- **Batch, habituate and automate your tasks.** I learnt this one from Tim Ferris, author of 'The 4-Hour Work Week'. Any regularly occurring work gets turned into a habit, something I do at a fixed time on a fixed date. Prepare to buy back loads of time with that one!

For instance, I plan my day every morning; work on my blog every Sunday afternoon; and I write first thing in the morning, batching together tasks where possible, eg. working on a series of blogs together.

Habit-based scheduling for regular work makes it easier to tackle irregular projects and creative ideas. It also prevents highly stressful schedule-busting pile-ups.

This approach of using routines to do the same thing at the same time every day also reduces the number of **decisions** you need to make, which are a big source of mental tension and stress. Similarly, you can use **technology** to automate routine tasks to save you time, for example setting up direct debits to minimise the time spent paying bills each month.

This also applies to email (as stated earlier), which I check and respond to only a couple of times a day, and rarely at night or on weekends.

- **Start early.** On certain projects that I know are important, I don't tolerate procrastination. When you know that you've already done three hours of work by 9.30am, the rest of the day runs a lot smoother!

Often, the hardest part of any task is getting started, so just start – the task is most often not nearly as bad as you thought it was going to be!

- Use technology to help you organise your time and locate the tools and information you need when you need them. From talking to many people over the years, one big common stressor is simply the ability to capture and **recall the things that they need to do.** They fear that they are going to forget something important.

Examples include:

- Evernote - this is one of the best tools for getting things out of your head. It allows you to capture notes in all formats (web screenshots, photos, emails, text, etc.). This enables you to get on with your current tasks knowing that you haven't lost your brilliant inspiration, or the next item on your 'to do' list. It is also fully 'tag-able', and therefore searchable.

- For those who need a task manager that will work for both your personal to-do lists and team collaboration, **Remember the Milk** (RTM) - is a slick and snappy web-based task management tool, with loads of great features, that syncs across a large number of devices, operating systems and web applications.

RTM works with iOS, Windows or Android phones, Google Calendars, Outlook, Evernote, Twitter, etc. You can also email tasks to it, which is really handy (and the original reason I went for this one). I've used RTM since 2008 and I now run both my professional and my personal life with it.

It has made such a difference to my stress levels and the only stress I now feel is worry that it will be cyber attacked!

- Delegate – you don't need to do it all yourself! The Internet makes it very easy to inexpensively find help, such as a virtual assistant to support you administratively for a few hours a week, or people to come over and fix broken door handles or other odd jobs. Crowdsourcing tools such as Elance and Checkatrade are great resources to find help.

- Finally, track how much TV (or other time guzzlers like gaming) you're consuming each day. Just 30 minutes less each day will give you 14 extra hours per month! Like any skill, the ability to switch off needs to be practised.

For additional reading, there are some great books and resources available on Time Management such as 'Eat that Frog' by Brian Tracey; 'The 4-Hour Week' by Tim Ferris; 'Getting Things Done' by David Allen, as well as regular podcasts such as 'Beyond the to do list.'

According to Laura Vanderkam, author of 168 Hours: You have more time than you think. Software today makes it very easy to apply these principles efficiently on a day-to-day basis.

BE DISCIPLINED

"Some feel that fear is okay as a lifestyle because they've heard that the meek shall inherit the earth. So they can go on with being meek as a way of life. They become soft-spoken and compliant, never standing up for themselves; always resigned to being a fluffy doormat. But scholars now say that in the scriptural texts that were translated from the Greek, the word praos doesn't exactly mean "meek" as people have always thought. In fact, it is more accurate to say it means "disciplined." A very big difference in those translations. It's much more encouraging to now realise that the disciplined shall inherit the earth."

- Steve Chandler

One skill that is synonymous with success is 'grit', the ability to keep going. In a study by the Marketing Leadership Council, of attributes most associated with success across leading corporate organisations, **grit** topped the list above agility, creativity and other skills usually associated with success. Like a marathon, those with the strongest stamina and the ability to adjust their path to find a better route, but always in a forward direction, achieve success.

Darren Hardy, in his book 'The Compound Effect', talked about 'Big Mo', that is, the amazing power that momentum brings. Momentum takes a lot of time and effort to get going, but once you are in the flow, things start to bring positive results. As soon as you stop doing your project and go on vacation or lose focus and move onto another project, Big Mo dies and you have to get it back all over again!

IT DOESN'T HAVE TO BE PERFECT

Many of us are not content until a project is truly 'perfect', devoid of a single flaw.

However, 'perfect' is incredibly difficult (and time consuming) to accomplish, requiring huge amounts of energy reserves. Indeed, the strife for perfection can be laden with anxiety and could be the path to depression, addictive practices (to block out the pain and stress) and indeed can lead to all sorts of missed opportunities (due to either a lack of time or energy to take on new projects).

As Brené Brown said in her book 'The Gifts of Imperfection', ask yourself is it really necessary to achieve perfection, or will 'really good' do just as well?

A SIMPLE METHOD TO GET THE MOST OUT OF YOUR DAY

IMPROVE

Improve your environment - spend time organising your workspace so you know where things are. Find a place for keys, shoes, wallet, phone, passports etc. so that you don't waste time and suffer unnecessary stress hunting for them!

PLAN

Plan your day by listing the things you need to do (using software or a notepad). Put them in order of importance based on potential outcomes and results.

TRACK

Become aware of time-wasting activities - interruptions like phone calls, emails, unfocused meetings, TV – track them using tools like Rescue Time.

DELEGATE

Decide what you need to do yourself and what can be delegated – get help if you need it.

PRIORITISE

Decide what needs to get done today, next week, next month and add to automated calendars for reminders; decide what doesn't need doing after all, and drop them from the list

Your mountain of tasks are now in some sort of order which should help you control them.

POSITIVE SELF-TALK

Use affirmations to alter your thinking, for example. 'Things are happening as they should, 'I have enough time to do everything I need to do' or an all-encapsulating 'I am truly grateful for my life'.

CELEBRATE

Give yourself rewards each time you achieve something, in order to keep you motivated. Teresa Amabile and Steven Kramer in the Progress Principle teach us to celebrate the "small wins" on the path to ultimate success, even if it's just a mental 'pat on the back'.

Keep going! Tenacity wins in the end.

Remember, you are ultimately in control

8 CONTEMPLATIVE HABITS

TAKE A BREAK

We've already talked about the importance of getting the basics right by exercising your body, upgrading your nutrition and getting sufficient sleep. Now it's time to move up a gear and focus on some other good, healthy habits that will serve you well and help you become more resilient.

As we go through the ideas, you may already be doing some of them, but it is important to take five days to track how often you actually do them and the benefits they bring, to see what is working and give you the space to try out other techniques.

TAKE A BREAK DURING THE DAY

You can't go at 100 miles per hour all day long. Whatever the activity, you need to build in time to take breaks throughout the day to rest your mind and re-energise your body. If you go non-stop, you risk burning out, which will force a longer break and impact your productivity.

Also, by changing your focus, you allow your subconscious mind to start working - and that's often when new ideas and solutions appear.

TAKE A LONGER BREAK

'The idea of taking time out of our busy lives to rest, dates back to the Ten Commandments."
– Ariana Huffington

No matter how busy you are, it's also a very good idea to build in long weekends or longer vacations to relax, rebalance your life and give you a fresh perspective. If it's hard to take a break in the middle of a project, plan to take some time off once it's over.

Occasionally, you may need to step back and sense-check the actual path that you're on. The end of each decade in your life is always a good point to pause and reflect.

When I hit my last significant birthday a few years ago, I headed off with my family to Australia for a couple of months. It was a fantastic experience and, more importantly, enabled me to do a significant 'deep dive' of my life. The benefit of being temporarily outside of it, allowed me to really fashion it exactly the way I wanted it.

On my return, I was amazed at how stressed everyone seemed to be, and was able to hold onto this state of calmness for several months, armed with my new plan of action.

TAKE A BREAK FROM YOUR MIND

'Calm mind brings inner strength and self-confidence, so that's very important for good health'.
- Dalai Lama

Sometimes you don't actually have to go anywhere to deflate stress. Treat yourself to a vacation that's all in your head by just learning to *relax.*

When life is busy, it can often be difficult to take time out to chill, but remember the relaxation response helps balance out your stress response, by decreasing your heart rate, blood pressure, rate of breathing and muscle tension.

Mastering practices like meditation, yoga or qi gong will greatly help you relax your mind and body and are based on thousands of years of practise and refinement.

MEDITATION

'Meditation is a reboot for your brain and your soul.'
- **Padamasree Warrior, CTO of Cisco**

'When you find peace within yourself, you become the kind of person who can live at peace with others.'
- **Peace Pilgrim**

'Wisdom is knowing we are all One. Love is what it feels like and Compassion is what it acts like.'
- **Ethan Walker III**

When you meditate, you focus on the present moment, which, as we said earlier, is all that really matters. It gives you control over your emotions, helping you reduce your stress, build your resilience, feel happier and generally let go.

This isn't just opinion, it has been validated by a number of studies - including one which put people who had never meditated before through an 8-week meditation programme and found that the meditation literally changed their brains (in a good way)!

So it's not surprising that in our increasingly stressful working environments, meditation is growing in popularity in the corporate world, moving away from its more 'new age', 'alternative' roots.

Meditation classes are now held at many major corporations, such as Medtronic, Apple, Google, Yahoo, McKinsey, IBM, Hughes Aircraft, Cisco and Raytheon.

Google's "Search Inside Yourself" programme has introduced mindfulness to more than 1,000 employees. And for seven years now, a growing number of General Mills workers have been practising meditation, yoga and mindfulness in the workplace.

There have been encouraging results: After one of General Mills' seven-week courses, 83% of participants said they were taking time each day to optimise their personal productivity (up from 23%); 82% make time to eliminate tasks with limited productivity value (up from 32%), 80% of senior execs reported a improvement in their decision-making ability, while 89% of them felt they became better listeners.

Other companies have also noticed improvements. For example Aetna (with Duke University School of Medicine) found that employees practising an hour of yoga per week decreased stress levels by a third, lowering individual healthcare costs by an average of $2,000 a year.

If you're new to meditation, and are keen to get started, some useful resources to help you include: Deepak Chopra / Oprah (https://chopracentermeditation.com/), Jon Kabat-Zinn (http://www.mindfulnesscds.com/) or my current favourite Tara Brach http://www.tarabrach.com - have a listen to some of her free guided meditation mp3s. There is also a great app you can download called 'Headspace' (https://www.headspace.com/).

I only started meditating properly in 2011 and it's now a daily ritual for me that keeps me grounded and present. I find it especially useful in my moments of overwhelm, to help me recentre and approach things from a calm perspective.

If you're struggling to find an extra 10 or 20 minutes, a good starting point is to turn household chores like tidying up after dinner or making the beds into meditation in motion, paying attention in particular to the breath and how it flows in and out. When the mind starts to wander, gently bring it back to the breath.

The real power comes when you can notice the signs of stress building up and stop it in its tracks. All you have to do then is simply notice it, breathe and bring yourself back into the present moment.

Where do you feel your stress? Is it in the pit of your stomach, or do you get a headache or an aching back? Whatever you feel, learn the signs that are unique to you, to recognise and act upon them before they take hold of you.

Stress will come into your life, but just observe it, accept it is there and then let it go, knowing that you are the master of your life.

Sounds easy, but as you do this, your mind will push back, trying to hold onto your stress, and it will succeed if you let it. That's ok – you will just need to calmly go back to your breath and keep going.

Eventually, you will be able to go for longer periods before your mind steps in again.

Find a time to meditate that works for you. I tend to meditate not long after I've woken in the morning. This really is a wonderful way to start the day. Perhaps you can give that gift to yourself, too? How much time can you find to give your active mind a well-earned daily rest?

TAKE ACTION NOW!

Close your eyes and imagine you're in the most relaxing place you've ever been, or make up a place you've never been to, but would like to go to in the future. Notice everything you can about the experience. What can you see? How do you feel? What does it smell like? What does it sound like? What are you saying to yourself? What feelings of gratitude come to mind? The more vivid the picture you paint in your mind, the more your body will respond to the invitation to relax.

Remember, you can go to this place at any time in your mind's eye. Whenever you start to feel the signs of stress or anxiety or sadness building, you now have this haven to go to, that no-one need know about and no-one can take away.

It is your special place.

BREATHE

Breathing is one of the most basic and easy ways to make a stressful situation more manageable.

As Gary Mack from Mind Gym tells us,

"Oxygen is energy - it's juice. Oxygen helps relax muscles and clear the mind. When you hold your breath, you are creating pressure and a nervous feeling. Athletes who choke start to become nervous about being nervous. Anxious about being anxious. One psychologist says anxiety is excitement 'without the breath.' "

You can train yourself to breathe more deeply by taking 5 minutes of each day to practise taking the air in through your nose (rather than your mouth) and sending it deep into your lungs so that your stomach expands like a balloon (your lungs are so big that you can even train yourself to take in air into your back). If you feel your shoulders rising, you are shallow breathing and that will lead to more anxiety.

The more you practise deep breathing, the more it will come naturally to you the rest of the time; and if you are in a particularly stressful situation, you can subtly take 5 slow, deep breaths and calm yourself down in the moment.

YOGA

Yoga has been practised for thousands of years and there are many different techniques. Personally I like Bikram Yoga, which takes place in 40 degree heat. It's also possible to use desk yoga techniques. Find out more here: http://bit.ly/re-yogaposes

In our hyper busy lives when it feels like there aren't enough hours in the day, finding time to do "nothing" can feel like an impossible goal (with also a degree of guilt attached to it, as there is the tendency to think of all the things you should be doing). But, as world famous yoga teacher Donna Farhi writes:

'By not doing so much, we create natural pauses to reflect.'

You also refill your reserves in order to be more productive afterwards.

"Yoga does not remove us from the reality or responsibilities of everyday life but rather places our feet firmly and resolutely in the practical ground of experience. We don't transcend our lives; we return to the life we left behind in the hopes of something better."
- Donna Farhi

TAKE ACTION NOW!

This week, find 30 minutes in your schedule to do nothing – lie on the floor and listen to your favourite music, or go for a walk without a destination in mind.

Relax every part of your body in turn. Don't forget to only allow in positive, calming thoughts.

MASSAGE

Build in massage as a regular habit. There are many different types.

I trained in 'Kahuna', which is a Hawaiian massage originally only performed by priests, as a transformative massage during rites of passage. It is incredibly relaxing, utilizing the masseur's whole arm, using long, continuous strokes where the therapist moves around you with their hands constantly on your body. It is an amazing experience, if you ever get to try it – it truly connects mind, body and spirit together in a way I've never experienced before in massage.

You can also support yourself with self-massage. For instance, the Ayurvedic facial massage takes a couple of minutes each day. Simply using your middle finger, rub these points on your face in a clockwise direction: the middle of the chin, corners of the mouth, middle area between upper lip and nose, outer edges of both nostrils, centre of the cheek bones, temples and the space between the eyebrows.

Another great ritual to adopt is to keep a bottle of olive oil in your shower. After every shower, whilst still wet, massage the oil into your shoulders, arms and legs.

TAKE A BREAK FROM TECHNOLOGY

As I wrote at the very beginning of this book, thanks to high tech gadgets, our lives have tremendously improved in many ways.

However, one of the hidden costs is that work worries can spill into home life and vice versa, blurring these boundaries and increasing stress. According to a study of 1,367 working men and women in New York State (two-thirds of them parents), all were overburdened by a blurring of the divide between home and work. This of course was perpetuated by devices that bring aspects of work right into the home.

One solution to this is to have a 'digital detox' built into your routine for at least one day per week.

This may well sound impossible for many people – devices have permeated into every aspect of our lives, but to take a bre

9 HEALTHY RELATIONSHIPS & SELF EXPRESSION

SURROUND YOURSELF WITH POSITIVE PEOPLE

Having strong relationships is key to resilience, and a good support network of family, friends and colleagues can ease your troubles and help you see things in a completely different way. So make sure you put time and energy into relationships as these are the people who will help you through stressful times (and vice versa).

As well as the books we read, the biggest influences in our lives are the people that we come in contact with on a daily basis. Jim Rohn, the famous entrepreneur and motivational speaker, famously said that we take on the characteristics of the 5 people we spend the most time with. So look around you and list the five key people in both your professional and personal lives.

When you're feeling down, do they help you frame the situation differently and find a solution, or do they make the problem worse?

The people in your life will have a significant influence on your mood and energy, so if you choose to hang out with pessimistic, cynical people, it will be hard to remain positive. Remember, you need supportive people in your life who are on a similar path to you, and can help you accomplish your dreams.

To determine who you are spending the most time with, use the Association Evaluator, a useful exercise from 'The Compound Effect' by Darren Hardy (http://bit.ly/re-association). It will help you decide who depletes you in some way, and guides you to find the people who you should be spending more time with.

If you're looking to expand your network, then consider joining local groups focused on topics that you are interested in, as that's where you're likely to meet like-minded people. To find local groups in your niche, check out www.meetup.com.

When life throws up challenges and problems for you that you don't know how to solve, first reach out to the people who care about you. If you don't feel comfortable, or are not in a position to discuss the problem with family, friends or colleagues, don't suffer alone.

Over the years, I have found that the 'reality' in your head is often not real at all. You can save yourself a huge amount of stress and anxiety by just articulating your thoughts and fears to someone who can provide a different perspective and will help you find solutions.

For bigger issues and challenges, consider working with qualified coaches and mentors who can guide you and challenge you to think differently. It will save you a lot of time, and also give you confidence in the direction you're heading. A good starting point to find a life coach is via personal referral, but failing that here's a good resource: www.lifecoach.com

History shows us that the groups who survive the longest do so because they form strong social groups, feel 'part of something', are valued and help each other (source: Outliers). We are social creatures and spending time with trusted people is an important way to deal with stress and promote health and wellbeing.

Whether you're an introvert or an extrovert, we all need each other.

THE IMPORTANCE OF SOCIAL WELLBEING

In the New York Times article 'The Island Where People Forget to Die', a Greek war veteran Stamatis Moraitis lived in the US from 1943.

In 1976 (in his mid 60's) he was diagnosed with lung cancer and given just 9 months to live. In this desperate state, he decided to go to Ikaria, the Greek Island of his ancestors, to live out his final days.

However, over the months, being nursed by his wife and mother, he started to feel a little better, so used to venture to church on Sundays. Then his old friends would come over, talking for hours over a bottle of wine. Then, his strength improved, he worked in his vineyard, gradually building that into a thriving business.

By some miracle, his cancer healed imperceptibly without any medical intervention, arguably due to the lifestyle he'd been living; one based on community, a very relaxed approach to time, lots of hill walking, plenty of naps, and plenty of home-grown food and wine.

At the time of the interview, Stamatis was 97 years old. Twenty-five years after moving to Ikaria, he went back to the US to ask his doctors why they thought he'd recovered from his advanced cancer – and they were all dead!

There are a lot of lessons that we can learn from this story – but the one that stands out the most for me is the importance of social community.

The more we feel a part of something, the more contented and happy we are.

WRITE IT DOWN

A massive help over the years for me has been daily journalling. Just pouring my thoughts out of my head and onto paper has provided perspective, clarity and direction and an opportunity to examine my life and gradually let go of the things that are bothering me.

Another technique that is similar to journaling is 'morning pages'. This is a process where you, every morning, write down what's in your head in an unstructured way.

This type of venting will enable you to vocalise your thoughts, releasing stress, and not creating more stress by worrying about being judged by someone else. It gets what's troubling you out of your head so that you can stop dwelling and start moving forward.

If you're interested in finding out more about the Morning Pages Technique, then I recommend Julia Cameron's excellent book, 'The Artist's Way'.

BE CAREFUL OF THE WORDS YOU USE

If you can, try to avoid using words like 'should' and 'must' – these are very loaded words and have heavy stressful burdens attach

10 BALANCE YOUR LIFE

FEEL FULFILLED IN YOUR WORK

If you're happy at work, it has a knock-on effect on the rest of your life.

Take a look at how you spend your workday. Do you enjoy your day? Does it interest you? Does it play to your strengths? Does it fulfil you? Does it match your values and the way you work? Does it challenge you without being too difficult? Are you in the right environment for you? With people that you enjoy working with? With appropriate remuneration?

It is possible to spend your day doing work you love, which energises you so much that it doesn't actually feel like work.

A couple of great books for ideas on career changes, is 'What Colour is My Parachute' by Richard N. Bolles and 'How To Get A Job You Love' by John Lees.

BOOST YOUR FINANCIAL WELLBEING

Money worries usually come out on top of the list of stressors.

We're living through economically challenging times where many of us have borrowed up to our eyeballs and can't afford the lifestyles we have chosen to lead. Luxury items such as TVs, phones, tablets, cars and holidays have become a necessity and we're forced to keep working just to stand still.

If that's true for you, take a step back and think about your 'financial wellbeing' which is made up of the amount you earn from all sources: the amount you spend and the amount you're able to save every month for 'a rainy day', or what Tony Robbins calls 'the freedom fund' (which is a lot more pleasant way of looking at it!) If you need help to analyse your spending patterns in order to simplify things, boost your income or plan for your financial future, Tony Robbin's book 'Money – Master the Game', is a great resource where you'll learn the money lessons that only the richest people in society know.

Also, if you need more handholding, and would like to work with a financial coach, I've worked with Wise Monkey Financial Coaching (www.financial-coaching.co.uk) in the past - they've really helped me with making some key decisions (and quickly saying no to certain ideas).

11 OTHER THERAPEUTIC PRACTICES

WE ARE MORE THAN OUR PHYSICAL BODIES

More and more scientific and medical studies are being released that support the view that we are in fact one big mind, body, spirit entity, and that there is a definite connection between our emotions and physical health.

Although science can't explain it, studies show that certain emotions are known to be associated with pain in certain regions of the body. These are consistent irrespective of age, sex or nationality. For instance, chest pain for those suffering from depression; whilst fear, anxiety and shame are all experienced in the gut.

There is some evidence to suggest that probiotics (beneficial bacteria) can have a direct effect on brain chemistry, thereby improving feelings of anxiety or depression. So perhaps one day, probiotics will be used as an alternative to antidepressants!

One mind-body therapy that takes the interrelationship between our emotions and physical health into account is the Emotional Freedom Technique (EFT).

EFT has lots of parallels to traditional acupuncture, making use, for instance of the same energy meridians. However, the key difference is that it doesn't use needles, but instead uses gentle tapping with your fingertips to transfer kinetic energy into specific meridians in your head and chest whilst you think about your specific problems, and voice positive affirmations.

The idea is that this combination of tapping the energy meridians and voicing positive affirmations work together to clear the emotional blocks, and restore your mind and body's balance, which are important for optimal health. Indeed, clinical trials have shown EFT to be able to rapidly reduce the emotional impact of incidents that trigger emotional stress.

For more information on EFT, look at http://eft.mercola.com

BODY STRESS RELEASE

A person with body stress may feel tense, tired and lacking in energy and enthusiasm for life. Headaches, backache and indigestion may follow. Alternatively, they may not feel any pain or stiffness, but have come to accept that they have less than 100% wellbeing. Tense muscles put pressure on nerves, which disturb the body's communication system and reduce the efficiency of the natural healing process.

According to practitioner Paul Masureik, 'Body Stress Release' (BSR) uses information provided by the body to determine where stored tension is undermining the efficiency of the nervous system and disturbing the body's ability to co-ordinate its functioning.

The practitioner locates stress by using the body as a bio-feedback mechanism.

Gentle pressure tests are conducted, working along the client's spine and other areas of the body. Once the sites of body stress are located, the practitioner releases the tension by hand, using light but definite pressure. Certain areas may feel quite sensitive; however some people find the releases so relaxing that they fall asleep.

The body may let go of locked-in tension rapidly but if stress has been stored for a long time, more releases may be required over a period of time. This is because the tight, protective layers of muscle tend to relax back to their normal tone in stages.

When I've had the treatment myself in the past, I've always felt absolutely fine after the treatment, apart from a feeling of intense fatigue for the following two nights; the kind of deep tiredness that can only be cured with sleep!

**What I really like about BSR is that it's truly holistic in the
sense that the BSR practitioner appreciates the need to treat
the whole person to find the source of the pain, rather than
just the part of the body that hurts.**

If you're interested to see whether BSR could help you, contact
Paul Masureik (http://www.bodystressrelease.co.uk) if you're
based near Lightwater, Surrey in the UK, or Annabel Boys
(www.unlockmyback.com) if you're near the South Coast, or to
the BSR site (http://www.bodystressrelease.org.uk), which lists the
qualified practitioners around the UK.

12 STRESS IN THE WORKPLACE

TIPS FOR EMPLOYERS

As we have been saying, stress is a big problem for individuals, and is therefore a huge problem for employers. Much has been written on the cost to business and industry through absenteeism due to stress, and these staggering stats are enough for any employer to take stress management seriously.

What I always find interesting is that it is the seemingly small acts that often make a huge difference to staff morale.

- Communication – business tends to be very fast moving and pressurised and few can be sure of their job security – a good communication strategy keeps employees informed, and alleviates a lot of worry.

- Giving feedback. Related to the communication point, it is important to give individuals constructive feedback, so that they know a). whether they are doing a good job or not, and b). how they can improve and grow (something we all want to do).

- Asking for feedback and for opinions. People often feel powerless over the content of their jobs and appreciate the ability to feed into the way their organisation works. You know yourself, if you feel that you have a say in work-related decisions, you're going to feel much more engaged.

- Having a team spirit. We are social animals and we like to hang out with like-minded people. So team drinks and fun events are really important for morale and team spirit.

- Undertaking a 'stress risk review' to identify sources of stress and other problems. Based on this insight, you can take action to minimise stress-related illness, staff turnover and poor performance. Methods of assessing risk include DIY methods such as online surveys to identify the issues, or focus groups, which work particularly well when there are known issues.

- A common stressor in the workplace is poor management. In fact for more than 60% of employees, their immediate manager is the most stressful aspect of their job. Targeted management training can make a big difference.

- Introducing a helpline for employees – there are a number of Employee Assistance Programs available, which provide a 24/7 helpline and face-to- face counselling for employees during hard times. These are not only for work issues. Relationship problems, money worries, health issues, etc., will all spill into work and employees need people to talk to who can listen and guide. This will ultimately result in more happy, productive employees.

- Educating and training staff on practical strategies to build their resilience, reduce negative stress levels and learn how they can spot the signs of stress. Workshops, tracking devices and other tools are all available and can help to understand issues that run through teams. Somerset County Council, for instance, found that training employees on stress-related issues resulted in a return of £5 for every £1 spent.

- Organising initiatives that bring teams together, benefitting their physical, emotional and community wellbeing. Many big companies are increasingly organising wellbeing events and programmes, largely enabled by wearable technologies that take the pain out of manually capturing data.

For instance, RELX Group, the Anglo-Dutch information company that owns RBI, runs a global wellbeing competition, fit2win, which encourages employees to establish fitness teams to compete for cash prizes for the charity of their choice.

Teams compete in four categories: running, walking, swimming and cycling. Live leader-boards spur competition. In 2013, 79 teams ran, walked, cycled and swam a total of 73,382 miles.

- Changing the office environment. Just like rearranging rooms and moving furniture around at home can be uplifting, it's exactly the same in offices.

Many traditional businesses are completely redesigning their workspaces to support today's more collaborative working styles, whilst also supporting the requirement for individual thought and creative work. These have led to 'third spaces': community areas that are neither work nor home, such as cafés and lounges. A great example is Google's offices around the world, that are designed to be 'home from home', supporting its employees to be creative and productive.

Giving employees permission to 'let it out' by punching a ball, squeezing a stress ball, or screaming at the top of their lungs. Students at Michigan State University, for example, always scream at midnight during finals week. Expressing stress relaxes the body.

13 SUMMING IT ALL UP

IN SUMMARY….

Learning to relieve stress quickly won't happen overnight. Like any skill, it takes time, self-exploration and, above all, practise. With practise, you can learn to spot your unique stressors and stay in control when the pressure builds.

Stress reduction mastery increases steadily the more you do it - think of it as a muscle that builds with repetition. It is also important to get better at dealing with our minds, quieting the chatter and living in and enjoying the present moment.

Having read this book, you now have access to a great toolkit, which, if applied, will help you build your resilience, free yourself up and channel the stressors in your life in a more productive way. The key is to resist trying to do everything at once. Explore the different techniques at your leisure, select the ones that work for you and then gradually build them into healthy habits.

Remember, you really are in control of your life and you can accomplish more than you ever thought possible. So, decide what life you really want for yourself and then go get it, but don't forget to enjoy the journey!

And please, do get in contact and share your thoughts about this book and any outcomes that have come from it. I am very keen to hear your feedback and celebrate your successes with you!

You can reach me on:

https://twitter.com/RawEnergy100
https://www.facebook.com/rawenergy.info
Lawrence@rawenergy.info
http://www.rawenergy.info

#successwithoutstress

'We have the power of choice over all, but two things - we must die and we must live until we die'

REAL STORIES:

HOW PEOPLE COPE WITH STRESS

'I go outside. There's something about natural light that is tremendously soothing to me.'

'First take a deep breath, or two. Remember, even if you can't control the event causing stress, you do have some control over your response to it. As an old Yiddish saying goes, 'You can't control the wind, but you can adjust the sails.'

'My most effective stress relief comes from speaking with friends, but only the ones I know have my best interests at heart. They are great listeners, supportive and almost always come up with strategies to cope with the stressor.'

'Get regular exercise and vary your exercise routine to prevent boredom.'

'Music is a great tool for stress relief. Pop on your headphones and listen to something that will transport you somewhere else.'

'There is only the present moment. If you fill your cup with past regret and future anxiety, there is no room for anything else.'

'Whenever I feel anxious in a meeting, I stay connected to my breath and squeeze the tips of my thumb and forefinger together.'

'I spend 10 minutes per day tidying.'

'I work standing up to get more blood pumping.'

'I surround my desk with pleasant images.'

'I focus on the worst case scenario and realise that it will be fine.'

'As a perfectionist, I have worked hard to understand what 'good enough' is, as this tendency put me under even more pressure. Brené Brown's book 'The Gifts of Imperfection', made a big difference to me, helping me understand that perfectionism is not the same thing as striving to be the best and can often be the path to depression, anxiety, addiction and life-paralysis, missing opportunities through fear of putting something out in the world that could be imperfect'.

HOW MUCH DO YOU INVEST IN YOURSELF AND YOUR WELLBEING?

- Do you have a high vegetable content in your diet?

- Do you eat organic produce where possible and use minimal chemicals at home?

- Do you use high quality supplements to support your digestive system?

- Do you drink 8 glasses of water / vegetable juice per day?

- Do you take time to move your body?

- Do you have regular chiropractic, reflexology and massage treatments?

- Do you take time for your family and friends?

- Do you have down time, where you can fully unwind? Do you laugh often?

- Do you make time every day to express your gratitude for the gifts you already have?

- Do you invest in coaching and education to support personal and business development?

APPENDICES

Appendix 1: How to give up smoking

Some great resources are: http://www.nhs.uk/smokefree and http://www.allencarr.com (both my brother- and sister-in-law gave up more than a decade ago, using Allen Carr's method)

Appendix 2: How stressed are you?

http://www.stress.org.uk/stresstest.aspx

Appendix 3 : How to melt stress and live longer

Notice and acknowledge the discomfort

Relax and release it no matter how urgent it feels – let the energy pass through you before you attempt to fix anything

Imagine sitting at the back of your head watching your thoughts, emotions and behaviour with detached compassion

Then ground yourself, connect to the present moment, feel the earth under your feet, smell the air

BIBLIOGRAPHY

Feel the Fear and Do it Anyway. Susan Jeffers
A Bug Free Mind, Andy Shaw
The Compound Effect, Darren Hardy
Mindful London. Tessa Watt
Drive, Daniel Pink
Sugar :Sickly or Sweet. Lawrence Mitchell
The Stress Management Societywww.stress.org.uk
Perfect Health. Deepak Chopra
You can Heal your Life. Louise Hay
Yoga for Runners .Lexie Williamson
New Scientist
Money: Master the Game: Tony Robbins
Thrive: The Third Metric to Redefining Success and Creating a Life of
Well-Being,
Wisdom, and Wonder
Thrive: Thrive: The Vegan Nutrition Guide to Optimal Performance
in Sports and
Life: The Whole Food Way to Lose Weight, Reduce Stress, and Stay
Healthy for
Life by Brendan Brazier
http://www.hsegov.uk/stress - HSE Management Standards
http://www.stress.org.uk- The Stress Management Society
http://www.isma.org.uk- the International Stress Management
Association UK
https://www.healthy-workplaces.eu/en/get-involved/how-to-get-
involved
http://www.humanstress.ca/stress-and-you/workers-and-
stress/burnout-vs-depression.html
http://www.standtoreason.org.uk/home.html. Stand to Reason
The Power of Now, Eckhart Tolle
The Bible
Bond, Galinsky, and Swanberg 1998
Health & Safety Executive
www.bbc.co.uk

'Management Standards' and work-related stress in the UK: Policy background and science" Colin J. Mackay, Rosanna Cousins, Peter J. Kelly, Steve Lee And Ron H. McCaig

www.nhs.uk/Conditions/stress-anxiety-epression/Pages/understanding-stress.aspx

http://www.humanstress.ca/stress/understand-your-stress/types-of-chronic-stress.html

www.healthcentral.com/anxiety/c/1950/30437/history-term-stress/

www.humanstress.ca/stress/what-is-stress/history-of-stress.html

http://www.helpguide.org/mental/stress_management_relief_coping.htm

http://psychcentral.com/blog/archives/2011/07/11/10-practical-ways-to-handle-stress/

http://www.nhs.uk/Conditions/stress-anxiety-depression/Pages/reduce-stress.aspx

http://www.wikihow.com/Deal-With-Stress

10 Practical Ways to Handle Stress, By Margarita Tartakovsky, M.S.

http://www.mayoclinic.com/health/coping-with-stress/SR00030/NSECTIONGROUP=2

http://www.psychologytoday.com/blog/the-race-good-health/201212/4-healthy-ways-cope-stress

http://www.webmd.com/balance/stress-management/stress-management-relieving-stress

http://www.webmd.com/balance/stress-management/stress-management-avoiding-unnecessary-stress?page=2

http://www.medicalnewstoday.com/articles/145855.php

Professor Cary Cooper, University of Lancaster

http://www.uhs.wisc.edu/health-topics/mental-health/healthy-way-to-handle-stress.shtml

http://www.wikihow.com/Deal-With-Stress#Treating_Stress_with_Lifestyle_Changes

http://www.mayoclinic.org/healthy-living/stress-management/basics/stress-basics/hlv-20049495?_ga=1.4300283.917659247.1423658527

http://www.psychologytoday.com/blog/in-practice/201301/17-psychology-experts-share-their-best-stress-relief-tips

http://www.humanstress.ca/stress/trick-your-stress/fight-or-flight.html

http://www.helpguide.org/mental/quick_stress_relief.htm

http://www.goodhousekeeping.com/health/wellness/stress-relief?link=rel&dom=wmd&src=syn&con=art&mag=ghk#category1-1

http://lifehacker.com/5976310/nine-strategies-successful-people-use-to-overcome-stress

http://www.wikihow.com/Face-and-Overcome-Stressful-Situations-Easily

http://www.mindtools.com/stress/rt/Application.htm

http://advancedlifeskills.com/blog/10-ways-to-overcome-stress/

http://www.cot.org.uk

http://www.greenster.com/magazine/9-stress-true-self/

http://thesecretyumiverse.wonderhowto.com/how-to/10-weird-ways-de-stress-0141424/

http://myfootpath.com/mypathfinder/4-unusual-stress-management-techniques-finals-week/

http://www.aolnews.com/2011/04/01/procrastination-found-to-be-an-effective-way-to-deal-with-stress/

http://www.parents.com/parenting/moms/healthy-mom/10-weird-ways-stress-makes-you-sick/?page=1

http://www.goodhousekeeping.com/health/wellness/stress-relief#category1-1

http://lifehacker.com/5945018/to-succeed-forget-self-esteem

http://lauravanderkam.com/books/168-hours/manage-your-time/

http://www.careershifters.org/

http://www.nhs.uk/Conditions/stress-anxiety-depression/Pages/stress-relief-exercise.aspx

http://www.wholeliving.com/134086/benefits-b-vitamins

http://www.livestrong.com/article/23155-b-vitamins-stress/

http://www.besthealthmag.ca/best-you/mental-health/8-nutrients-to-help-beat-anxiety#EDTO2r3WuAv2EQS2.97

http://www.besthealthmag.ca/best-you/mental-health/8-nutrients-to-help-beat-anxiety#EDTO2r3WuAv2EQS2.97

https://www.psychologytoday.com/articles/200304/vitamin-c-stress-buster

http://www.prevention.com/mind-body/emotional-health/13-healthy-foods-reduce-stress-and-depression?s=7

http://www.todaysdietitian.com/healthandnutrition/health/fight-stress-with-food.shtml#sthash.iw3BDGuo.dpuf

http://en.wikipedia.org/wiki/List_of_antioxidants_in_food

http://www.sagepub.com/upm-data/38637_Chapter1.pdf

http://www.apa.org/research/action/immune.aspx

http://www.garysturt.free-online.co.uk/theostre.htm

https://www.psychologytoday.com/blog/high-octane-women/201205/where-do-you-fall-the-burnout-continuum

http://www.ncbi.nlm.nih.gov/pubmed/23426535

http://www.kiki-health.co.uk/articles_beware_of_borrowed_energy.asp

Charlotta Hughes www.bemelifecoaching.com

LIST OF STUDIES

Unum. Research from the financial protection firm argued that employees who feel well cared for are 27% more likely to stay with their current employer for more than 5 years, compared with those who feel only adequately cared for

Zurich. Found critical illness is one of the biggest risks faced by small and medium sized businesses, with almost two-thirds having no protection insurance in place for their owners and key employers

Cigna. Found that more than 57% of employers polled provided OH, with 63% offering EAPs and 53% providing private medical insurance

CBI and Medicash showed clear business benefits for supporting employee health and wellbeing. The report 'Getting better: workplace health as a business issue' set out ways in which businesses can improve staff wellbeing and develop 'joined-up' health and wellbeing programmes

Capita. A survey by Capita found that nearly half (47%) of employees say they know a colleague who has quit because of stress.

Unknown source. One study found that commuters in London have as much cortisol as fighter pilots

Eunice Kennedy Shriver Institute. Found that women with the highest stress levels were half as likely to conceive as the women with the lowest levels.

The European Agency for Safety and Health at Work's (EU-OSHA) publication. Found that • 72% of workers felt that job reorganisation or job insecurity was one of the most common causes of work-related stress; • 66% attributed stress to worked or workload'; • 59% attributed stress to 'being subject to unacceptable behaviours such as bullying or harassment'; • 51% of all workers reported that work-related stress is common in their workplace; • around four in ten workers think that stress is not handled well in their workplace.

Unknown source. Research shows that those who travel in an active manner see an average productivity boost of 12.5% and have significantly fewer sick days. Healthy employees are also 47% more alert and make 27% fewer errors than those who are inactive.

Wake Forest University. Found that meditation lowered pain intensity, and another study found that meditation can actually increase the thickness of the prefrontal cortex region of the brain and slow the thinning that occurs as we age, impacting cognitive functions.

University of Washington. Found that HR managers who had gone through an 8 week mindfulness and meditation course were able to concentrate for longer stretches of time, were less distracted and had lower stress levels.

University of Essex. Found that 94% of mental health patients who were prescribed exercise saw mental health benefits.

Great British Sleep Survey. Found that poor sleepers are 7 times more likely to feel helpless and 5 times more likely to feel alone. Also found that the average Brit goes to bed at 11.15pm and gets 6 hours 35 minutes sleep per night.

Scientists at Surrey University revealed that 7 days of poor sleep can disrupt hundreds of genes linked to stress, immunity and inflammation

Robert Suposky of Stanford University. Found that a baboon's stress levels was dependent on rank. The higher the rank, the lower the stress. Lower ranks also had higher blood pressure, elevated levels of stress hormones, an impaired immunity system, and an impaired reproductive system, so position in the hierarchy makes a difference.

The Whitehall Study. Found parallels to the Baboon study in British Civil Service, ie. those people at the top had lowest risk of heart disease; and lower abdomen fat. They also found a correlation between stress levels and illness levels.

Unknown source. Found that mothers of young, disabled children experience more stress as you'd effect and that this chronic stress impacts their general wellbeing, leading to, for instance premature ageing. However, they also found that support groups and in-joke humour had healing benefits.

Google. Found that enabling employees to graze all day on healthy snacks made a big difference to their productivity in the afternoon, rather than having a heavy meal.

Harvard Medical School. Found that deep relaxation changes our bodies on a genetic level. Researchers found that, in long-term practitioners of yoga and meditation, far more disease fighting genes were active, compared to those who practised no form of relaxation. In particular, they found genes that protect from disorders such as pain, infertility and high blood, joint pain pressure were switched on. They called the effect 'The relaxation effect'

Academics from Loughborough University identified six resilient qualities that enable high achievers to excel in demanding contexts:

1. Positive and proactive personality, including openness to new experiences, conscientiousness, optimism, and honesty to oneself.

2. Experience and learning: being confronted with potentially stressful situations and learning from such incidents was perceived to provide a vital foundation for resilience and thriving.

3. Sense of control: being able to recognise their active choice to operate in demanding environments, possessing the ability to prioritise activities, and positively respond to unpredictable circumstances.

4. Flexibility and adaptability: able to solve problems creatively, react positively to change, remain politically aware, and display emotional intelligence in a variety of situations.

5. Balance and perspective: being able to understand the importance of achieving an optimal work-life balance and retaining a broad sense of identity that was not too focused on a career-related role.

6. Perceived social support: perceiving that high quality social support was available to them from colleagues and mentors as well as from family and friends.

Unknown source. One study involved diaries of 180 catholic nuns from the School of Sisters of Notre Damn, all before 1917. As young women, all asked to write down their thoughts in biographical journals. More than 5 decades later, researchers mined their entries for positivity. Found nuns who had written most overtly joyful content lived as much as 10 years longer than nuns who were neutral or more negative.

Studies in the United States and Europe have repeatedly shown that when addicted people are taught to meditate, their level of anxiety decreases, pulling down with it their use of alcohol, cigarettes and other drugs. These studies have supported the hypothesis that simply by reducing stress and anxiety and raising the level of inner satisfaction, can motivate addicts to stop their habits. One study, for instance, among two-year meditators, found that 92 percent had decreased their use of marijuana and 77 percent gave it up entirely. A similar study found the same results with alcohol.

Studies of happy people have found common characteristics, including having a full social life, looking on the brighter side of life; a strong sense of self-worth and an ability to live in the present and not dwell on the past. They also found that whilst genetics will play a part in how happy people are, life circumstances only contribute 10%, whereas interesting activities accounts for 40%.

FURTHER REFERENCES

http://www.hsegov.uk/stress- HSE Management Standards which Tools to help employers work together to prevent excessive work-related stress

http://www.stress.org.uk- The Stress Management Society which includes a quick stress management checklist, useful tips on stress reduction

http://www.isma.org.uk- the International Stress Management Association UK who have introduced a Charter for wellbeing and Performance at work.

https://www.healthy-workplaces.eu/en/get-involved/how-to-get-involved

http://www.standtoreason.org.uk/home.html. Stand to Reason is a registered charity offering courses and consultancy focused on managing stress, building resilience and increasing team productivity, tackling stigma and changing workplace culture.

http://healthland.time.com/2011/10/20/what-does-a-400-increase-in-antidepressant-prescribing-really-mean/

http://www.stress.org/americas-1-health-problem/

http://www.visionarylead.org/articles/spbus.htm

DISCLAIMER

This guide is for informational purposes only.

I am not a doctor, lawyer or accountant, and any advice I give is my personal opinion based on my experience and previous studies and is only for educational purposes. You should always seek the advice of your doctor before acting on something that I have published or recommended.

The material in this guide may include information, products or services by third parties. Third Party materials comprise the products and opinions expressed by their owners. As such, I do not assume any responsibility or liability for any Third Party materials or opinions.

ABOUT THE AUTHOR

Lawrence Mitchell is a life and wellbeing coach, raw foods enthusiast, distance runner and marketing professional. He's currently Director of Marketing and Wellbeing for Reed Business Information, a large information and publishing company, and founder of Raw Energy, a wellbeing education and coaching service, created to help people regain control of their personal health through education, food awareness and physical activity.

https://twitter.com/RawEnergy100/
https://www.facebook.com/rawenergy.info
Lawrence@rawenergy.info

http://www.rawenergy.info

If you enjoyed reading this book, please review it on my Amazon page http://bit.ly/rawenergy-sws
Thanks very much for sharing!

QUICK ORDER FORM
Satisfaction guaranteed

Email orders: lawrence@rawenergy.info
Telephone orders: call +44 1372 469234

Order by post:
Please send the following books, discs or courses. I understand that
I may return them for a full refund - for any reason, no questions
asked.

See our website for FREE information on other books, speaking,
seminars & one to one / group coaching

Name:

Address:

Tel:

Email:

Amount sent (£5.99 per copy, plus £4.50 UK postage – please
contact us for latest prices / costs for international delivery)

Credit card number:
Name on card:
Exp. date:

Send form to: 2 Claremont End, Esher, Surrey, KT10 9LZ, UK
http://www.rawenergy.info